most fragrant
Japanica Hearne

Morning Sun
winter spring

Japonica
Sasanqua Tail

MW01291387

CAMELLIA
GARDEN
FIELD GUIDE

Forrest S. Latta
Brenda C. Litchfield

Written by Forrest S. Latta and Brenda C. Litchfield
Illustrations by Chuck Higginbotham
Photography by Forrest Latta and Brenda Litchfield

Copyright © 2015
Printed and bound in the United States of America. All rights reserved

Although the authors have made every effort to endure the accuracy and completeness of information contained in this book, we assume no responsibility for errors, inaccuracies, omissions, or any inconsistency herein. All slight of people, places, or organizations are unintentional.

First printing January 2005
Second printing January 2008
Third printing November 2015

Contents

Introducing Camellias

Under cover of darkness on a December night, disguised in native Indian garb, some American colonists avoided notice as they paddled the cold waters of Boston Harbor. Climbing aboard a British-flagged ship of the East India Company, only one thing was on their mind – *Camellia sinensis*! Known popularly as "tea," nothing symbolized the Crown and Parliament more than the crushed leaves of this venerable plant -- which they gleefully dumped overboard. A plant that inspired a revolution!

In a twist of irony, the New World's liberation extended to the cousins of those same tea plants, which soon acquired status as naturalized citizens on U.S. soil. Americans had acquired not only the Europeans' taste for tea, they also laid claim to a royal treasure dating back thousands of years to Oriental dynasties whose botanical family tree now extends down to us in the form of today's beautiful winter-blooming camellias.

The camellia's legacy contributes much to its appreciation and this book is written, in part, to share its story and explain in practical terms how today's camellias can be enjoyed by anyone -- even if only admiring blooms over a cup of tea.

Camellia plants live for hundreds of years, faithfully producing magnificent blooms for each generation during the fall and winter months. They are grown as shrubs, trees, and even ground cover. Tidy evergreens year-round, camellias seldom need pruning and rarely drop leaves. And nothing beats camellias for ease of maintenance. Even without their amazing winter blooms, a plant of such distinction would be highly valued for its handsome landscape presence. Does Earth have another plant that can make all those claims?

This book is written for two main groups: first-time camellia buyers who seek basic advice on choosing and growing these plants, and new owners of old camellias who seek guidance in restoring, maintaining, and enjoying their inherited wealth. To the experienced grower, we can only ask indulgence, as the book's content will be familiar. One may even have different tastes and techniques than offered here, but no matter. That is one of the most enjoyable things about camellia gardening -- discovering what works for you.

The *Camellia Garden Field Guide* is the product of collaboration in its truest sense. Yes, it expresses our own subjective point of view, from years of successes, discoveries, trials, and tribulations. Without it, such a book would hardly be more than a dull technical manual, on par with the tax code for entertainment. It also, however, reflects the shared experiences of our camellia friends on the Gulf Coast, especially those who support the collections at Bellingrath Gardens and Mobile Botanical Gardens (the K. Sawada WinterGarden), two outstanding public gardens where camellias occupy a place of honor.

So much more can be written about camellias than space allows here, but fortunately an array of excellent books and articles exists on the fine points of camellia growing. A partial list of book suggestions is offered in a later chapter. For those who seek more personalized advice, we encourage you to connect with one of the many local and national camellia groups, which are ready sources of up-to-date advice and information.

Finally, if camellias interest you we highly encourage you to consider joining the American Camellia Society, which annually publishes *The American Camellia Yearbook* as well as a beautiful and informative quarterly magazine. It also hosts a robust website that contains a photo gallery of camellia varieties and an extensive on-line library. Membership in any of these groups may prove to be your best garden investment.

PREFACE

The Story of Camellias in America

From Tea to Shining Tree

Some of the greatest discoveries in the civilized world have happened purely by accident: Columbus bumping into America, scientists finding a use for silly putty, and Europe encountering camellias. Did someone say camellias? Yes, the flowering aristocrat of European conservatories, northern arboreta, and southern gardens actually began its Western reign as the butt of an Oriental joke.

It began in the early 1600s as Europeans got their first taste of these evergreen shrubs when missionaries returning from the Far East to England brought back a beverage brewed from dried leaves. The leaves were from *Camellia sinensis*, which became known as tea. The drink became popular, initially for its medicinal benefit of stimulating without intoxicating. It was a rare find; a medicine that tasted good! As the popularity of tea drinking increased, so did demand for tea leaves.

English merchants, seeing an opportunity for greater profits, reasoned that growing their own tea could reduce costs and eliminate dependency on Chinese suppliers, so they ordered a shipment of plants. Chinese merchants, equal to the English regarding the bottom line, filled the order for camellia plants – with one slight twist. They substituted *Camellia japonica* rather than *Camellia sinensis*! The English soon discovered that the joke was on them, as this different species did not brew into a robust quaff! It did, however, produce sensational flowers.

This amazing new plant quickly quenched English gardeners' thirst for winter blooms, and interest in camellias spread through Europe like royal gossip. Indeed, Europeans treated these new arrivals like nobility. Camellias became the rage of Paris and the darling of Victorian England. They preceded two-car garages as symbols of wealth and status. Privileged families of Europe were evaluated by the number of camellias in their hothouses.

These Oriental stowaways soon were celebrated as continental celebrities. Artists painted them, fashionable ladies wore them, and authors wrote about them. In 1852, Alexandre Dumas penned *La Dame Aux Camelias*, which was set to music the following year by Verdi in his popular composition *La Traviata*. Nurserymen fortified the celebrated plant's regal bearing by naming new introductions after princes, barons, ladies, and any other noble personage. So passionate were the English about these plants, in an 1845 letter Queen Victoria wrote, "If we have no mountains to boast of, we have the sea, which is ever enjoyable, and we have camellias...."

But as the tides of history teach us, strong ebbs follow great crests, and the wave of camellia popularity that washed over Europe began to recede. What influences precipitated this, or why camellia interest has always seemed to swing in cycles, is a riddle one can only chuckle and scratch his head over.

Legend claims that the first plants of *Camellia japonica* in America arrived in New York Harbor in the late 1790s. They were bound for John Stevens, the founder of Hoboken, New Jersey, delivered by an English nurseryman named Michael Floy. Floy's home was in Devonshire near Exeter, a major English nursery center. In 1800, Mr. Stevens received another plant said to be the first white camellia, 'Alba Plena.' Floy meanwhile launched a commercial nursery in New York's Bowery Village which later moved to Harlem.

Although these were the first *ornamental* camellias to cross the Atlantic, they were not the first camellias to arrive here. Every grade school student can recount the event of December 16, 1773, when colonists outfitted in Indian garb boarded a British-flagged ship of the East India Company and dumped an entire shipment of tax-laden *Camellia sinensis* leaves (tea) into Boston Harbor to protest "taxation without representation." Who knew that such an amusing prank would inspire a national revolution, and fewer still have connected that iconic event with today's garden camellias. Yes, history has had its share of laughs with camellias!

As early as 1772, tea plants were being shipped to Savannah and Charleston where tea plantations were started by merchants seeking a home-grown opportunity. For various reasons, the tea-growing enterprises failed. But, *Camellia japonica* did not fail. Just as in Europe years before, camellias captured the New World's interest. Nurserymen and florists began importing more plants from Europe. New York and Boston became camellia hubs where plants were grown primarily for cut blooms. By the 1840s the center for camellia activity shifted southward, but not far. Philadelphia became the new cradle of camellias, producing so many plants that its nurseries were shipping excess inventory back to Europe and to the American South.

But these northern cultivars were not the South's introduction to camellias. Southern lore contends to its dying day that camellias arrived in Charleston and Savannah before the earliest shipments to its northern neighbors. Precisely when the first plants arrived is uncertain, but what is known is that by 1830, large collections of camellias were flourishing at Magnolia Plantation and Middleton Place near Charleston. There they could grow freely outdoors in the southern soils and climate. It was a mutual acceptance on both ends, for excited southern gardeners welcomed camellias as though they were lost children returning to their rightful homes. It is interesting when surveying the history of camellias to realize that their presence in the pre-Civil War South was relatively short and not widespread, yet they quickly became a symbol of grace and charm in the old South.

Around 1850 camellias began heading west, as did so many other immigrants seeking land on which to grow. A former Boston resident, James Warren, shipped plants to his new home in Sacramento, and by 1853 he was advertising them for sale in the newspaper. Though the camellia failed to inspire the same epidemic frenzy as the Gold Rush, popularity was high in California and camellias migrated both southward and up the coast into Oregon and Washington.

By 1860 camellias were becoming a part of life in the United States, but that soon ceased. The Civil War and the period of Reconstruction uprooted any desire for growing camellias, possibly because times were so hard and camellias were so inedible. Fascination with camellias did not bloom again until the early twentieth century. But those southern gardens that survived war's devastation and Reconstruction's ruin were home to proud collections of camellia treasures. One of the few post-war commercial producers was Belgian-born P. J. Berckmans of Fruitland Nurseries, whose property later became the site of today's Augusta National Golf Course. (Some of the old plants remain.) Another was Langdon Nurseries near Mobile, established in 1853 by Charles Langdon who later served as Mayor of Mobile and a founder of Auburn University.

Many of the keepsake plants of the nineteenth century remain some of today's favorites. They include varieties shipped from Europe such as 'Donckelarii,' 'Adolphe Audusson,' 'Herme, 'Bella Romana,' 'Lady Clare,' 'Elegans,' and 'Pink Perfection,' plus some early introductions from Magnolia Plantation of Charleston: 'Mathotiana' (Purple Dawn), 'Duchess of Sutherland' and 'Debutante.' Perhaps because of historical association, or just that they reminded later generations of their grandparents' gardens, those classic varieties held – and still hold – a timeless appeal.

By the early 1900s a new era of camellias was dawning and new pioneers in camellia development were busy at work. The riddle of camellia popularity was laughing again. Shipments of Japanese camellia plants and seeds were arriving on both the West Coast and Gulf Coast bound for energetic nurserymen like K. Sawada and Gus Gerbing in the South and Toichi Domoto in the West, who were again producing new varieties. This early part of the twentieth century saw new gardens built and existing gardens expanded, many specializing in camellias. Descanso and Huntington Gardens in California became famous for their vast numbers of camellias. Large collections were assembled in Pennsylvania's Longwood Gardens, Norfolk Gardens in Virginia, Maclay Gardens in Tallahassee, Bellingrath Gardens in Mobile, Orton Plantation near Wilmington, and Jungle Gardens in Louisiana. Anchoring these collections were large camellias – 50 years and older – purchased and transplanted from old plantations and home sites.

The pendulum of camellia interest was in full swing again and enjoying popularity greater than ever. Communities began having camellia shows (Boston held its first in 1829), camellia clubs, camellia balls, and camellia festivals. Some especially proud camellia meccas designated themselves "Camellia Cities," starting with Sacramento in 1908. The State of Alabama named it the state flower. At the end of World War II some camellia enthusiasts in the South decided to meet in Savannah to form the American Camellia Society in 1945. Camellia appeal had gone national!

By the late 1940s demand for camellias stampeded past available supply. Nurserymen went into heavy production to fill larger orders and to satisfy the outcry for new varieties. A one-gallon plant in 1950 sold for a higher price than it does now. By the end of the 1950s, camellias had reached the pinnacle of their popularity. Camellias had become more than garden plants; they were social events. Camellia shows were such major attractions that in 1957 the Birmingham show (60,000 visitors) outdrew the "Iron Bowl" between Alabama's two football powerhouses. In the city of Chicago the toniest restaurant was the Camellia House at the Drake Hotel, which featured camellia décor on every surface including its flatware. Excitement over the country's favorite plant gave new meaning to the term "camellia culture."

In the 1960s, however, the cycle swung again; the romantic glow began to fade, and the clock struck midnight at the camellia ball. Harsh winters resulted in poor blooming seasons and interest in winter's favorite flower waned. Suddenly there was a surplus of nursery stock, and plants that sold for a premium a few years earlier wouldn't raise a buyer's eyebrow. There was a new feeling in the country, a new era in America, the Age of Camelot. Camellias no longer had a seat of honor at the table. There were new interests, such as television, space travel, Elvis, and the Beatles drawing a new generation of Americans indoors and away from their parents' garden paths.

In many ways the camellia's fall from grace was the fault of those who promoted it so much. Growers had saturated the market with so many new varieties that camellia collectors became dizzy. Camellia shows, once friendly affairs where neighbors freely shared scions and tips, became highly competitive arenas where specialty growers, most believing that bigger was better, dazzled spectators with ever larger blooms, especially flowers of the species *Camellia reticulata*. Many of these were generally unavailable at nurseries, required greenhouse protection, and would not grow easily outside the spectators' kitchen doors. The amateur gardener was feeling left out.

But you can't keep a good plant down, and camellias survived this decline in interest. Some nurserymen ceased growing camellias, but most merely cut back production. They especially quit struggling to grow as many varieties, limiting their efforts to stronger cultivars that rooted easily and bloomed well. They continued to experiment in their greenhouse laboratories, producing new hybrids that would again capture the attention of the public. In the past few years, different species have been crossed in hopes of creating a new spectrum of camellia colors: yellows, blues, and pastels. Efforts are ongoing to hybridize fragrant and cold hardy species with camellias that bloom profusely. Some of the new hybrids are hardy as far north as USDA Zone 6. A newly discovered summer-blooming species, *Camellia azalea*, holds the promise of year round blooms in the near future. One thing about camellias, there is never a dull moment.

Lastly, an account of camellia history is not complete without reference to how the plant got its name. It was devised by Carl Linnaeus, the leading botanist of his day, to honor a Jesuit missionary named Joseph Kamel who spent most of his life running a clinic for the poor in the Philippines. It was Linnaeus who developed the binomial system of plant nomenclature still used worldwide, and in 1735 he published *Systema Naturae* in which he gave this venerable plant the Latinized version of Kamel's name. However, although Kamel was an amateur botanist, it is thought unlikely he ever saw a camellia. That may be the best laugh of all!

Adapted from an original article by George Wright. Used with permission.

 # Camellia Icons

Like national flags, symbols are often used by governments as a public relations tool to promote allegiance and common identity. States and cities use them to convey something attractive about their culture or geography. It thus is no surprise that one American state and several cities have adopted the camellia as an official symbol.

Alabama is the Camellia State having declared it the state flower in 1959. The capitol building in Montgomery features a camellia arboretum and its state quarter depicts camellias on the reverse side. The "state flower" legislation was signed by Governor John Patterson whose wife Mary Jo was raised near Greenville, one of

America's Camellia Cities.

Other "Camellia Cities" of note include:

Sacramento, California – The state capitol where camellias first arrived on the west coast and which hosts an annual camellia festival and parade. The capitol building is surrounded by hundreds of huge camellias.

Fort Walton Beach, Florida – A charming beach town and seafood mecca where a former First Lady founded the local camellia club and was instrumental in the nickname.

Quitman, Georgia – Home of "Betty Sheffield," whose likeness is captured in a bronze statue that presides over a public park in this famously charming camellia town.

Slidell, Louisiana – A colorful city on the shore of Lake Pontchartrain that hosts a very popular Camellia Ball each year, crowning a Camellia Queen and King.

McComb, Mississippi – Home of "Mississippi Blues" music, Britney Spears, and the self-proclaimed "greatest variety of camellias in America."

Newberg, Oregon – Near Portland in the Willamette Valley (Oregon's wine country) where you can sip Oregon Pinot and attend the city's annual Camellia Festival in April.

Did You Know?

What hall of fame sportscaster was known for his weekly conversations about camellias on National Public Radio? Red Barber, the longtime voice of the Detroit Tigers, who raised camellias at his home in Tallahassee.

Some of the finest camellias on the market are "field grown" in full sun along the central Gulf Coast, where they are planted and grown in rows like farm crops, until they are dug and sold "balled and burlap" or "B&B" as referred to in the nursery trade.

In Japan and China, wild camellias historically were often harvested to burn as coal in the fireplace. Camellia wood is so dense, it produces a very hot fire.

Camellia wood is among the densest on Earth producing wood that is far denser than the Live Oak tree, whose life span is about one third that of the camellia.

There was once a time in Alabama when the annual Birmingham camellia show equaled or exceeded the "Iron Bowl" (the football game between bitter rivals, the University of Alabama and Auburn university) in attendance, attracting around 50,000 people.

The "Camellia House" was once the name of the fashionable dinner club in what famous Chicago Hotel? The Drake. It was filled with camellia décor, including flatware, carpet, drapes, and may other items.

Where Camellias Grow

Feels Almost Like Home!

It is no secret to American gardeners that many of our favorite plants (and more than a few invasive nuisances) are naturalized citizens that emigrated from other lands, including the camellia. But the camellia itself may not be in on the secret, for while it is not native to North America, it feels very much at home in many regions!

The key to understanding where and how camellias grow is to first understand their native habitat. The camellia is an indigenous forest plant in southern Japan and the coastal provinces of China where the climate is warm and temperate. This region features relatively mild winters, with summer months experiencing above average rainfall and high humidity. Its soil is slightly acidic (loose forest mold) and well-drained because of its natural slopes. These same conditions also are conducive to azaleas, hydrangeas, and other plants of Asian origin.

Wherever these conditions are most closely duplicated, camellias will thrive outdoors. This, however, is a very general statement because certain factors can be compensated and the traditional Camellia Belt is continually expanding as more cold-hardy hybrids arrive on the market.

In the United States the camellia's natural climate is generally found in three main regions: (1) the Pacific Coast from British Columbia to Southern California; (2) the Gulf Coast from East Texas to Central Florida; and (3) the Atlantic Coast from Central Florida to New York. These regions often are referred to as the "Camellia Belt." (See Figure 1 below.) They generally feature warm summers and relatively mild winters, allowing camellias to be grown outdoors with little problem. While all these areas do not offer ideal growing conditions, camellias may still be grown outside with proper attention.

Figure 1. The traditional "Camellia Belt"

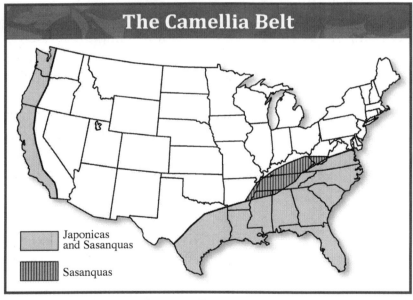

While humidity is generally beneficial, camellias are successfully grown in some dryer parts of California, such as Sacramento, where the average summer humidity is relatively low. In those areas, camellias require plenty of water during the growing season, including the fall months. Other areas may lack ideal soil or drainage, which may be remedied by appropriate soil amendments and planting them high, or in raised beds. In areas that experience extremes of cold temperature, camellia growers adapt by selecting hardier varieties and planting them in locations that offer some shelter from the cold north wind.

Generally speaking, camellias can normally withstand winter temperatures down to 5° F with little or no permanent damage although ripened buds may be ruined. The risk of injury to the plant itself occurs when the mercury drops very suddenly, which does not allow for temperature acclimation. Camellia growers in the coldest regions may even use a greenhouse or temporary shelter for winter protection. There are new cold hardy hybrids that can withstand outdoor temperatures down to -10° F and still bloom! These new cold hardy varieties have extended the range of the Camellia Belt northward to USDA Zone 6.

Camellias actually need a certain amount of heat and cold to bloom properly. For instance, studies have shown that a camellia must have at least a few days of temperatures 80° F or above for bud initiation, and that longer exposure to summer heat actually produces larger blooms. By the same token, camellias must have at least a few days in the 40° to 50° F range to properly open their buds, especially the more complex blooms such as rose-form or formal doubles.

If the weather is consistently temperate, such as the higher elevations of the Big Island of Hawaii, which lacks extremes of heat and cold, camellias still make gorgeous foliage plants and the single red varieties bloom with little problem. However they sometimes have difficulty opening the formal double blooms depending on the weather, due to insufficient extremes of heat and cold.

These climatic differences also explain the variations in certain camellia blooms of the same variety in different parts of the world. Certain camellias may bloom very differently in Europe or Australia than in the United States. Likewise there can be variations among different regions within the United States. For example, a formal double such as 'Sea Foam' or 'Pink Perfection' may bloom poorly in parts of Southern California or Central Florida, failing to open fully, whereas those same varieties are outstanding 200 miles north. This is one of the intriguing things about camellias; they seem to have a "personality" of their own and may exhibit a unique form in your garden.

Understanding these climatic differences also helps in troubleshooting. A common cause of bud drop (also known as bull nosing) can be an unusually dry summer and fall, due to lower rainfall and/or humidity, leaving the plant without enough water to service the needs of bud development. This results in dry and crunchy buds that fail to open. Certain formal double varieties may need more hours of cold temperature, causing the buds in a mild climate to open only partially, leaving an unopened rosebud center. Another example is the soils of many southeastern coastal areas, which are naturally acidic but sometimes too acidic for certain varieties to grow well. Yet another example is a colder climate where a plant may lack sufficient water before the ground freezes, producing a drying effect that interferes with proper bud development.

The number of hours of sunshine is another major influence on camellia bloom production. A geographic region that gets more hours of sun will produce a greater number of larger flowers than a region with less. A Swiss garden, for example, gets approximately 2,200 hours whereas an English garden may get only 1,600. Alternately, an area with plenty of sunshine may experience a below average bud set during an unusually cloudy summer, and the flowers will be smaller than normal. For similar reasons, a plant that becomes shaded over time may exhibit spindly growth and produce fewer and smaller blooms.

Poor plant performance can often be remedied by thinning or removing some trees or relocating a plant within the same garden. It is not unusual, for instance, to move a poor performer to another spot – sometimes only a few feet away – where it gets more (or less) sun. Certain variations in soil pH, minerals, and drainage can also play a significant role in camellia performance, causing a plant to perk up when moved. A plant that receives no breeze (such as an enclosed courtyard) can be more susceptible to scale insects and spider mites, which can be remedied by moving it to a more open spot that is better ventilated.

Microclimates may dictate moving a formal double variety to a spot where it gets more hours of cold with favorable results. That may mean away from heated structures, or where it will receive more northern exposure, or even a low spot that gathers cold air. The reverse is equally true, as a plant that struggles in the cold north wind may benefit from the shelter of a windbreak or the warmth of a nearby structure. One gardener's spouse said he moves around plants like furniture! And there is an element of truth in that.

Herein lies one of the most interesting things about camellias; some are better suited for specific climates or locations, while others may perform consistently anywhere. And regardless where you live, you can artificially influence the blooming characteristics of an existing plant by where you place it in the garden. That is not to mention container-grown camellias, which may be moved around to suit a plant's preferences, through trial and error.

These factors should also be kept in mind when selecting camellia plants, as climate considerations may dictate which varieties perform best in certain locations. Unless you are knowledgeable (or adventuresome) it often is wise to copy what is being grown successfully nearby, or to check with an experienced grower to ask whether a certain variety is well suited for your locale.

Gulf Coast Camellias

Camellias arrived on the Gulf Coast in the early 1800s, with the first commercial records appearing in 1839 when a nurseryman named Gilbert Rotton settled in Mobile, Alabama, advertising about 50 varieties.

Langdon's Nursery established in 1853 near Citronelle, north of Mobile, listed in its 1890 catalog some 39 varieties. During the Civil War, the Mobile nursery C. V. Ravier and Sons established a florist business to import camellias from France for distribution and cut flower production.

Interest in camellias flourished on the Gulf Coast in the late 1800s and early 20th century, as camellias were planted extensively in fine residential landscapes and public gardens. The owners of large nurseries such as Overlook (K. Sawada) and Longview (Robert Rubel) stoked enthusiasm on the Gulf Coast and nationwide. Camellia specialty nurseries continued to appear until at one point in 1957 it was reported by Dr. Harold Hume that over one million potted camellias were in production in the Mobile area alone.

Public institutions soon planted camellia collections, such as at Spring Hill College, the Mobile Botanical Gardens, the University of Mobile, and the University of South Alabama. These joined Bellingrath Gardens where camellias already were famous. Many of the original plantings can be seen today, flourishing over 50 years later as a living time capsule.

Meanwhile in the early 20th century, camellia clubs were organized along the Gulf Coast, such as at Pensacola, Mobile, Gulfport and New Orleans. They soon began emerging in cities farther inland as well, in cities such as Atlanta, Baton Rouge, Birmingham, Columbus, Dothan, Greenville, Jackson, Montgomery, and Shreveport – places where camellias are very popular to this day.

 # Did You Know?

In the first half of the 1900s the market for older, mature camellias was so great they were often purchased (for sums in the hundreds of dollars) and dug from the yards and gardens of homeowners in the Mobile Bay area. They were shipped by rail car to Charleston and other destinations where they were transplanted in the gardens of estate homes.

What city in America currently has the largest market for camellias in the landscape? Atlanta. Most of the camellias grown on the central Gulf Coast are sold to the Atlanta market.

In the southern hemisphere (such as Australia and New Zealand) camellia blooming season coincides with our summertime, so camellias are literally blooming somewhere in the world at all times.

The Camellia Family

And the Shape of Things to Come

Imagine a monotonous world where all pet dogs looked alike. Thankfully there are Poodles, Dachshunds, Collies, and Retrievers – to name a few -- and even chance "hybrids" we know as lovable mutts!

Perhaps you have begun to realize that there are many different camellias too. Why does it matter? For some of us, any old dog will do. Others are more desirous of certain traits unique to a particular species. Because camellias are long-lived, and often do become like family members, knowing a little about their differences can greatly contribute to your satisfaction and enjoyment.

You may be interested to know, for example, that within the same plant family, the genus *Camellia*, you can find everything from small trees to dwarf shrubs. Some have large blooms, others small; some are fragrant, others not; some like cold weather, others hot. Some bloom in winter, while others open in spring or fall (and soon summer). Some even make a marvelous brew – known to westerners as "tea" – the world's most popular drink for centuries. In fact, you may have sipped the infused leaves of *Camellia sinensis* (tea) and not realized it!

That is one of the many fascinating things about camellias, the sheer number of unique species -- somewhere between 200 and 250 in all -- and more are discovered each year. Within each species are many different varieties, some numbering in the thousands, such as *Camellia japonica* which has over 5,000 known varieties. Japonica, you say? What's that? And sasanqua?

Yes, camellias have quite an extended family tree and knowing something about their special qualities is not only interesting, it offers insight into things to come. Plant breeders are hard at work, diligently combining the best characteristics of various species to create the "super plants" of tomorrow (and even today). For instance, a recently discovered summer-blooming species, *Camellia azalea*, offers the promise of year-round camellias, which are far along in the testing stage.

For the moment, however, the main camellia species from an ornamental standpoint are: (1) *Japonica*, (2) *Sasanqua*, and (3) *Reticulata*. Many gardens have specimens of each of these and some of their hybrids as well. Hybrids are even essential to outdoor growth of the Reticulata species, which is too tender in its pure form but hardier when crossed with a japonica. There also are many new cold-hardy hybrids that combine japonica with a species such as *Camellia oleifera*, which has survived the harshest winters. Many of the lesser-known species (some listed at the end of this chapter), while garden-worthy in their own right, are very popular for breeding and crossing varieties.

Japonica

Perhaps *Camellia japonica* is the species that comes to mind for most people when they hear the name, camellia. Japonica was discovered in Japan (the word itself means "from Japan") and was even once known as the Japanese

Rose. Japonica is also found in Vietnam, China, Korea, Taiwan, and other parts of Southeast Asia. The climate in that region is ideal for camellias, which live as indigenous understory trees in forests with climates very similar to our camellia belt.

Japonicas produce beautiful winter flowers that range in size from 1½ inches (miniature) to 5 inches or more (very large). Colors likewise range from pure white to dark red, and many have variegated patterns of mixed colors. Yellow camellias are still rare, but are increasingly available. While there is yet no orange or blue japonica, camellia breeders are working with newly discovered wild species to make controlled crosses to extend the color palate even further.

Japonicas, if left un-pruned, may grow into small trees. With their glossy green leaves, they add a lush elegance to any garden. The japonica's leaves also vary in shape, from round to narrow, and pointed to serrate. Some leaves are lobed and others look like fishtails. The foliage occasionally shows a yellow variegation, and some produce new growth in shades of red. Only a few japonica blooms are slightly fragrant, but given their beauty they don't really need it.

Sasanqua

Once regarded as inferior to japonicas, *Camellia sasanqua* was ignored for many years. In modern times, the sasanqua has become extremely popular for its landscape value as well as its prolific fall blooms, which often are fragrant. Sasanqua has been around for hundreds of years but once was more prized for its leaves and seed than its blooms. Today, some plants' leaves are still used in Asia to make tea and their seeds are crushed to produce seed oil for lubrication, lighting, cooking, and cosmetics.

Sasanquas produce an explosion of color during fall and early winter. Most of them bloom profusely and are breathtaking in full bloom. The flowers, while beautiful, do not serve well as cut flowers because they shatter easily, meaning the petals fall. This, however, can create a colorful carpet around the garden floor, enhancing the dramatic effect. One popular variety, 'Mine no yuki,' is popularly known as 'Snow on the Mountain' because of its snow-white petals which blanket the base of a plant in bloom. Nearly all sasanqua blooms have a slight fragrance, much to the delight of both humans and bees. When nothing else is blooming, sasanquas offer bees an abundance of pollen.

Amazing hedges can be created with sasanquas. They also can be trained into stylish espalier forms against a wall. They grow rapidly and usually tolerate full sun. When planted in mass, they are truly stunning to behold.

There now are many sasanqua varieties to choose from, in all shapes and sizes: low compact plants, or tall columnar shapes, and tall spreading ones as well. Some will grow 20 feet in height. Because they grow vigorously they often are used as rootstock onto which japonica cuttings are grafted. There literally is a sasanqua for every garden use, and they herald the beginning of camellia blooming season, which means japonicas are close behind.

Reticulata

From the Yunnan province of southern China came this relatively new species, *Camellia reticulata*, which has taken the camellia world by storm. It produces some of the largest and most spectacular blooms of anything in the gardening world. Its huge blooms can reach 8 inches wide! The blooms also often have fluted and swirled petals that are amazing to see. Many reticulata blooms are almost florescent in the vividness of their brilliant red or pink colors, seldom seen among japonicas or anything else in the gardening world for that matter. Retics (as they are commonly called) also tend to open later in the year, which helps stretch the camellia blooming season. And they respond well to gibberellic acid, resulting in even larger and brighter flowers often timed to coincide with holidays and camellia shows, making them especially prized among collectors and show enthusiasts.

The only drawback to retics is that many have an open and sparse growing habit, often described as a "coat rack" shape, making them less attractive as a garden specimen. Their leaves can sometimes be dull green, lacking the luster of a traditional japonica. But a retic's austere appearance is more than offset by its dazzling, large blooms. To compensate, retics often are grown in the garden as background plants, or grouped with others that disguise their lanky structure.

The word reticulata refers to the prominent veins or reticulated patterns in the leaves. In their original form, retics are finicky plants that can't tolerate much cold weather, and they respond poorly to heavy pruning. When crossed with a stronger species such as a japonica, however, retics can be quite hardy and grown outdoors with relative ease, much to the delight of the camellia world. Therefore most retics grown in gardens today are "retic hybrids."

Any of the retic hybrids would make an outstanding addition to your garden. For starters, three specimens that offer both a pleasing garden shape and sensational blooms are 'Dr. Clifford Parks,' 'Frank Houser,' and 'Valentine's Day.' Any of these will astound your friends and is sure to become your new favorite. Because a retic is only slightly tender compared to traditional japonicas, it is recommended you grow it in sunny location that will receive some shelter from the coldest winter wind.

Cold Hardy Camellias

Few things in the camellia world are as exciting as seeing them enjoyed for the first time by our friends in northern climates. Once limited to the so-called "Camellia Belt" or northern greenhouses, camellias now are finding homes in outdoor gardens farther north. Thanks to expert camellia hybridizers such as Dr. Clifford Parks (University of North Carolina) and Dr. William Ackerman (U.S. National Arboretum) new plants are being developed to withstand temperatures far below previous experience.

The cold hardiness of some of these camellias extends to USDA zone 6b where winter temperatures can fall to 5 degrees below zero. In the Camellia Belt, the normal blooming season extends consistently from fall through late spring, peaking in January and February. In northern areas, they start blooming in October, peak in November and some continue through December. Others begin blooming in early March and continue through May. Cold-hardy hybrids are better adapted to sudden and severe temperature drops.

Thanks to the new cold-hardy varieties, gardeners as far north as New Jersey and Ohio can now grow camellias outside. Many of the cold hardy varieties have names such as 'Winter's Fire,' 'Winter's Joy,' 'Winter's Cupid,' and 'Winter's Interlude' (all developed by Dr. Ackerman). Korean hybridizers have developed several with names like 'Korean Snow' and 'Korean Fire.' The cold hardy varieties benefit from being planted in a protected location, similar to retics: behind other plants, with houses as a windbreak, or in valleys. Check the ACS website for many more recommended cold-hardy varieties and sources.

New Colors

Ah, the elusive yellow camellia! Unless you add a yellow crayon to your wax (see chapter 14) you will rarely see a perfect bright yellow camellia. But hybridizers are making considerable progress. An outdoor bloom of 'Senritsu Ko,' for example, won the ACS national camellia show recently, stunning judges with its yellow petals edged in light pink. This and other new yellow cultivars are being developed by hybridization with wild yellow species recently discovered in China. There also are some exciting new hybrids from Japan. Day-by-day, experts are succeeding in transferring the yellow color to other species through cross-pollination. And with yellow now arriving, orange is not far behind.

Progress also has been made in producing a blue camellia. An example is 'Green's Blues,' a sasanqua hybrid that was originated by second-generation plantsman Bobby Green of Fairhope, Alabama. It is a bushy, low growing hybrid that initially opens as a red bloom but turns a shade of blue as it matures. Gene Phillips of Savannah, Georgia, likewise has been experimenting with yellows and blues, having organized a Hybridizer's Network that now includes a great talent pool of growers who are collaborating to produce new colors and varieties.

Other Species

There are many other species of camellias -- possibly as many as 250 -- but most are not readily available for gardens in the U.S. Many are found in the wilds of Japan, China, Viet Nam, Burma, India, and Hong Kong. These other species vary from small plants to those that grow over 20 feet tall. Blooms are usually small, single form flowers that vary from white to deep red. While these wild species may appear to be simple compared to their spectacular cousins, they are key to the hybridizing of promising new species.

The biggest news in the camellia world is the discovery in China in 1986 of a new species called the *Camellia azalea*. This is a unique species that has the traits of both a camellia and an azalea: nice, thick evergreen leaves and a brilliant red bloom similar to an azalea but with thicker petals. It is both sun and heat tolerant. The added bonus is that it blooms every month of the year!

Dr. Gao Jiyin is working on several projects with his research team in Fuyang, China using *Camellia azalea* as a parent for hybridizing and cross breeding. He has successfully crossed this sturdy plant with numerous japonicas with impressive results. The flowers he is producing are marvelous – comparable to any outstanding japonica bloom – and they open in summer amid considerable heat. It is just a matter of time before these new cultivars are available worldwide.

In addition to *C. azalea*, the following list includes some of the other better-known camellia species that are being grown both for their novelty and uniqueness and to encourage the development of hybrids.

C. senensis is the species that started it all! This is the tea plant that is so popular around the world. Every garden should have one. Origin – Southeast Asia.

C. hiemalis is the species that produces vigorous growers such as 'Kanjiro' and 'Rose of Autumn'. It also produces some dwarf varieties like 'Shishigashira'. Origin – China.

C. oleifera is the species that produces camellia oil. In breeding is it prized for its cold hardiness. It is the basis for most of the breeding program of Drs. Ackerman and Parks.

Origin – Southeast Asia.

C. rusticana as subspecies of japonica, known as the "snow camellia" because its native habitat is the higher elevations of southeast asia, where it often is covered in snow before blooming in spring as the snow melts.

C. saluenensis is valuable for its cold resistance, long blooming period, and prolific blooms. It is the source of Williamsii hybrids such as 'Donation,' 'Charlean,' 'Joe Nuccio,' 'Taylor's Perfection,' and others. It also is highly resistant to petal blight. Origin – Southern China.

C. vernalis is the parent of the beautiful 'Egao' series of blooms, as well as 'Star Above Star' and many other non-retic hybrids. Origin – unknown.

C. lutchuenensis is very fragrant. It is the main source of fragrant hybrids such as 'Cinnamon Cindy,' 'Scentuous,' 'High Fragrance,' and is a popular breeding species. Origin – Southern islands of Japan.

C. nitidissima is one of the exciting yellow species that is being used to create hybrids. It is the source of 'Senritsu Ko' and about a dozen other new yellow hybrids from Japan. Origin – China and Vietnam.

C. azalea is the new kid on the block and is being used to develop plants that bloom in the summer. Dr. Gao in China has produced 20 outstanding summer bloomers. Currently not available in the U.S. except to plant experts. Origin – Southern China.

With such a plethora of exciting choices in the camellia world, the main challenge to us camellia lovers is that we may eventually run out of space. Thank goodness for public gardens!

Registering New Camellias

Registering a new camellia variety is easy. The American Camellia Society offers this service for a cost of only $10.00. It is important to do your homework, as new registrations are reserved only for blooms that are distinctly different from all others.

A committee of accredited judges reviews each application, which must include specific details about its size and characteristics, much like a patent application. Two photos also are required. The particulars of this process are on the ACS website.

Once a new variety is registered, its photo and description are published in the American Camellia Yearbook as well as The Camellia Journal. This information is also added to the ACS website for general publication. A description is also sent to the editors of the *Camellia Nomenclature book*, the authoritative reference of all registered camellias grown in the United States.

It is noteworthy to mention that most "chance seedlings" and mutations are unexceptional, although often beautiful and worth growing in your own garden. With nearly 10,000 registered varieties (including 5,000 japonicas alone) the likelihood of discovering a distinct new one is rather small. One experienced grower estimated the odds as one in 10,000. In a controlled breeding program (where special varieties are hand pollinated) the chances may improve to one in 100.

If you are unsure about the merit of a newly discovered camellia variety, an expert evaluation can be obtained by entering it in a special camellia show division for seedlings and "sport" mutations. There, ACS accredited judges will closely inspect it, awarding ribbons to the best new ones.

 # Did You Know?

- Camellias are one of the rare plants that bloom while they are asleep. While camellias put on their buds during the growing season, the buds do not open until the plant is dormant.

- Camellias are nocturnal bloomers. Their blooms open during the night.

- The following colors are not found in any registered Camellia japonica varieties, at least not yet: orange, blue, green. But hybridizers are hard at work on these new and exciting varieties.

- So admired were camellias in the orient that some daring adventurist eventually tried to drink them, discovering to his delight (and probably relief) the pleasure we now take for granted in a cup of tea, which comes from the Camellia sinensis.

Did You Know?

Camellia seedlings are like humans: the offspring is never identical to the parents, but bears some of the characteristics of both.

The average time period for a seedling to bloom is 7 to 10 years.

Camellia seeds should be planted immediately after harvest. Their germinating capability declines if kept dry. Seeds kept in a plastic bag together with a moist paper towel can remain viable for up to a year.

According to the National Institutes of Health, oil from the seeds of Camellia oleifera has the potential to be a powerful anti-oxidant. Next to Camellia sinensis (tea) Camellia oleifera has become the second most economically important camellia grown on the planet.

Camellias can't stand wet feet. Their roots literally need air to survive, and extended water saturation will suffocate and kill them. Plant high!

Camellia Talk

How Do You Say "Camellia"?

As you travel the U.S. you may notice a funny thing. Not all camellia enthusiasts seem to agree on how to say its name! In fact, if you want to share a laugh at a camellia meeting, try asking someone this question: Do you say "ka-MEEL-ya?" Or do you say "ka-MELL-ya?" Depending on where you are, the answer may be different! How in the world could that happen? The answer, interestingly enough, dates back to when the camellia debuted on the Paris stage!

For the first 100 years after the camellia got its name, it invariably was pronounced ka-MELL-ya, emphasizing the second syllable, which rhymes with bell. That was the name assigned in 1735 by botanist Carl Linnaeus, who invented the world's Latin-based system of plant names. He chose it to honor a deceased Jesuit missionary named Joseph Kamel (pronounced ka-MELL) adapting the Latinized version of his name, Camellus. Linnaeus then assigned the names *Camellia japonica* and *Camellia sasanqua* to those species in 1753.

A century later, Verdi's famous opera *La Traviata* changed everything! Premiering in Venice in 1853, it was a masterpiece based on Alexander Dumas' immensely popular novel and play *La Dame Aux Camelias* (The Lady of the Camellias), which Verdi had seen in Paris. The English-speaking world soon shortened the French play's title to "Camille" (pronounced Ka-MEEL) which also was the title used in the famous 1936 American movie version starring Greta Garbo and Lionel Barrymore. Thus from the influence of Dumas' play, the world trended toward pronouncing camellia as "ka-MEEL-ya." Most modern dictionary scholars took note, adjusting their official preference to the long "e" sound, and widely abandoning the old pronunciation. See for example, Merriam-Webster's Collegiate Dictionary (Tenth ed. 1995). Some dictionaries still list it both ways.

To this day, however, many camellia fanciers insist that ka-MELL-ya is the only proper pronunciation, which in certain parts of the country has remained the custom. To others, it is more natural and familiar to say ka-MEEL-ya, hearkening back to Hollywood and the Paris stage. But no matter! You will be happy to know that either way is perfectly acceptable.

Like "tomato" or "pecan," the differences are mostly regional. The most common pronunciation in states along the Gulf and West Coasts is "ka-MEEL-ya," whereas gardeners in the Atlantic states (who were growing camellias long before Dumas' play) still say "ka-MELL-ya." Whichever way we pronounce it, we all agree on this: "camellia" is a word that should be uttered often! And we all get along charmingly.

Japonica

The word japonica, pronounced "Ja-PAH-ni-ka," means "from Japan." However, in some regions – particularly the Deep South – it is not uncommon to hear the word japonica in reference to all garden camellias, not just the species *Camellia japonica*. This custom probably endures from a time when folks grew up hearing the word japonica around the kitchen table in reference to their parents' or grandparents' garden camellias, which predated the introduction of new species and hybrids. It therefore has a time-honored cultural tradition in certain locales where, because everyone knows what is meant, it is perfectly acceptable and there is no need for correction.

Reticulata

Another word that camelliaphiles cannot seem to agree how to pronounce is "reticulata," a species gaining in popularity for its exceptionally large blooms. But your ears may be confused from hearing two different pronunciations. The traditional pronunciation for Latin derivatives like reticulata would be "re-tik-yoo-LOTTA." However, it is quite common to hear it pronounced "re-tik-yoo-LATE-a." The Latin version (with the LOTTA sound) is more popular on the Atlantic and Gulf Coasts, whereas our Pacific Coast friends (where reticulata first was introduced in the U.S.) seem to prefer the "LATE" sound. Again, either way is fine, whatever you are comfortable with.

Sasanqua

At least everyone agrees on this. The word "sasanqua," that popular and highly floriferous fall-blooming species, always is pronounced "sa-SAN-kwa" without any regional variation in meaning or sound. And what an enchanting sound it is!

Variety Names

Most modern camellia varieties, such as those developed in the last 50 years, are American origins so you seldom will have any problem saying their names. However, it remains true that some of the most popular camellias in America are of a vintage that predates their introduction into this country. Thus they still bear names given by their Japanese or French originators, who often named them for friends, places, and even royalty. These names can be tongue twisters for the newcomer who has never heard them pronounced.

The following is a short list of some of the more difficult camellia names and their proper pronunciations. Here again, there are certain regional and personal differences so don't be surprised.

Pronunciation of Camellia Varieties	
Adolphe Audusson	AH-dolf O-dew-sawn
Alba Plena	AL-ba PLEE-na
Arejishi	AHR-eh-JEE-shee
Chandlerii	CHAND-ler-eye
C. M. Hovey	C. M. HUH-vee
Daikagura	Die-kah-GOO-ra
Debutante	DEB-yoo-thant
Donckelarii	DONK-luh-rye
Elegans	ELL-eh-gahns
Fimbriata	Fim-bree-AY-tah
Gloire de Nantes	GLWAHR-duh-NAWNT
Guilio Nuccio	JOO-lee-o NOO-chee-o
Haku-rakuten	HAH-koo rah-KOO-ten
Hana-fuki	HAH-nah FOO-kee
Herme	HER-mee (not Her-mees)
Imura	IMM-erra
Iwane Shibori	Ee-WAH-nee SHIB-erree
Joseph Pfingstl	Joseph FING-stl
Joshua Youtz	Joshua YOOTS
Kanjiro	Can-JYE-roh

Kumasaka	KOO-mah-SAH-kah
Lady Vansittart	Lady Van-SIT-ert
Mathotiana	Mah-THO-tee-anna
Mine-no-yuki	MINN-ay-no-YOO-kee
Rosea Superba	Roh-ZAY-eh Soo-PER-ba
Shishi gashira	SHEE-shee gah-SHEE-rah
Ville de Nantes	VEEL- duh-Nawnt

For assistance pronouncing the names of older camellias of foreign origin, see the very excellent article "Pronunciation of Camellia Varietal Names," by Jessie W. Katz and Dave C. Strother, *American Camellia Yearbook*, p. 259 (1957).

 ## Stop and Smell the Camellias!

A four-foot tall little girl with a yellow-tipped nose marched up with a slight frown. "Why don't they smell?" she asked sadly. She, rather obviously, had smell-tested some show blooms before realizing something was amiss. Handing her a bloom of 'High Fragrance,' I saw her frown give way to a satisfied smile. All was forgiven.

"Dogs have odors, flowers have scents," a teacher once said in explaining the different words. I suppose something in our DNA makes us naturally expect flowers to have a sweet scent. We feel short-changed when they don't! But as someone once said, "God didn't think camellias needed fragrance" since they have no competition for bees in winter. Nonetheless, we all appreciate scented flowers.

Maybe that is why an old plant of 'Herme' won my admiration with its combination of fragrance and beauty. It's still one of my all-time favorites. About once a year, an Internet chat room will turn to a discussion of the best fragrant varieties. The funny thing is, few comments are about the flower's appearance. Most gardeners, it seems, will settle for a less spectacular bloom in exchange for an aromatic payoff. But occasionally we find one with both!

That is one reason hybridizers are hard at work. An article in the Los Angeles Times quoted Tom Nuccio (Nuccio's Nursery) describing 'High Fragrance' as, "on a scent scale of 10 – an 8 or 9." Other varieties that combine beauty and fragrance are 'Kramer's Supreme,' 'Scentsation,' 'Sweet Emily Kate,' 'Cinnamon Cindy' and others listed in Chapter 6.

My yellow-nosed friend and I are indebted to hybridizers who are exploring one of the main frontiers of camellia plant development – satisfying the expectations of gardeners who want both beauty and fragrance. Just imagine what will emerge in the next 10 years.

Choosing Camellias
Caution: May be Addictive

The first questions asked by most gardeners desiring to plant a camellia are, where can I find them and which ones should I choose? In most areas, options are often limited to a few selections at a local garden center, but they need not be.

A prime source is the local plant sale hosted by public gardens and camellia clubs. If there is a specific camellia variety you want, many nurseries have on hand a *"Plant Finder"* catalogue that lists wholesale nurseries that offer it, and they can place an order. Professional landscapers may also provide this service. Many outstanding camellia specialty nurseries will deliver plants by mail, which are ordered from catalogues and websites. And if all else fails, you can make or obtain a graft of the desired variety from a local gardener.

The fact is, all named camellia varieties are beautiful, but not all are alike. Like choosing a pet, it often helps to know their differences and whether a certain variety will suit your expectations. Large blooms or small; red, white or pink; columnar or spreading; fast growing or slow; upright or dwarf; cold tolerant or hardy; sun tolerant or shade; fall blooms or winter – these are only a few of the differences. And with so many varieties to consider (over 5,000 choices among *Camellia japonica* alone!) the process can be dizzying.

For one who is offered limited options at a local nursery

and is unfamiliar with the different variety characteristics, the discussion below may be useful for knowing what you are buying. One-gallon plants are cheaper, of course, but because camellias are generally slow growers (think of the pruning time saved!) it is often best to purchase a larger plant. Two-gallon sizes are ideal. Even larger plants are available wholesale for instant landscape impact.

Before purchasing a camellia from a nursery or sale, inspect it carefully. Choose plants with a label that lists the variety name and leave it on the plant until you can replace it with a metal tag. Make sure the foliage is healthy, and avoid any plants with obvious wilted or dead leaves or limbs. When buying a two-gallon or larger plant, look for camellias grown in a squat pot if possible – these are shorter, wider nursery pots designed for shrubs (as opposed to deep narrow pots). The reason is, it will have a root system better suited for transplanting because camellia roots grow shallow, not deep.

An all-around good garden variety is one that offers abundant blooms, handsome shape and foliage, dependable growth, and easy maintenance. It would be a mistake, however, to assume that all camellias have those features and are suitable for all conditions. Sometimes it is hard to resist the temptation to order every variety whose bloom catches your eye at a camellia show or in a nursery catalogue! Let prudence rule the day.

Recommended Japonicas

A helpful starting point in choosing camellias is a list of time-tested favorites. Like an index of blue chip stocks, it represents proven winners from a large number of options. You can hardly go wrong when selecting from this list. And veteran growers will nod in approval when you announce what you planted.

For the prospective camellia grower, here are some popular favorites compiled from a survey of growers with many years of experience. The growers first were asked to list the one variety no garden should be without. A few selections stood out above all others: 'Mathotiana' (Purple Dawn), 'Pink Perfection,' 'Debutante,' 'Professor Sargent,' 'Lady Clare' and 'Magnoliaeflora.' These are classic varieties found in nearly every camellia collection and always make a good choice.

The survey also asked the veteran growers to name their ten personal favorites giving special attention to *proven performers* along the U.S. Gulf Coast. Here are the results, ranked in order:

Camellia Japonica Suggestions	
First Fifteen	**Second Fifteen**
Mathotiana (Purple Dawn)	Grace Albritton
Pink Perfection	Helen Bower
Alba Plena	Junior Prom
Debutante	Lady Clare
Betty Sheffield Supreme	Magic City
Ville de Nantes	Melissa Anne
Black Magic	Tomorrow
Mathotiana Supreme	Kramer's Supreme
Carter's Sunburst	Cherries Jubilee
Dr. Tinsley	Herme
Edna Bass	Drama Girl
Magnoliaeflora	Fircone
Professor Sargent	Margaret Davis
Buttons 'n' Bows	Mary Agnes Patin

Next is a list of Camellia japonicas that have been selected by the American Camellia Society as "Hall of Fame" varieties. These are outstanding camellias that have proven themselves over time and won the universal acclaim of serious growers for both their garden value and spectacular blooms.

American Camellia Society Hall of Fame Japonica Varieties	
Adolphe Audusson	Magnoliafloria
Alba Plena	Man Size (miniature)
Betty Sheffield	Mathotiana (Purple
Carter's Sunburst	Dawn)
Debutante	Pink Perfection
Donckelarii	R. L. Wheeler
Drama Girl	Reg Ragland
Elaine's Betty	Sawada's Dream
Elegans (Chandler)	Showtime
Grace Albritton	Showman
Guilio Nuccio	Tiffany
Lady Clare	Tomorrow

The above lists are not all encompassing but are an excellent starting point if you wish to plant a few camellias, or even for the more experienced grower wishing to evaluate an existing collection. Are these the "best" varieties you could own? That is debatable, as "best" is a matter of personal taste. And therein lies the fun – deciding which camellias are your personal favorites.

Sasanqua Varieties

In addition to japonicas, many growers enjoy other camellia varieties as well, the most popular alternative being the species *Camellia sasanqua*. While sasanqua blooms are smaller, the plant's greatest advantage is that it grows faster, blooms more heavily, and – above all – it blooms in the autumn. In fact there are few plants that stop traffic like a sasanqua in full bloom. For gardeners who are interested in adding this species, here is a partial list of outstanding sasanquas that thrive in most camellia climates:

Popular Sasanquas	
Bonanza	Rosea
Chansonette	Setsugekka
Daydream	Shishigashira
Jean May	Showa-no-sakae
Kanjiro	Sparkling Burgundy
Leslie Anne	Stephanie Golden
Mine No Yuki	Yuletide
Pink Snow	

Fragrant Varieties

Everyone loves a fragrant flower, and while the *Camellia japonica* is generally not known for its fragrance, there are many varieties that are. In fact, some gardeners specialize in fragrant varieties and species. Bear in mind, however, that nearly all fall-blooming sasanquas are fragrant, as well as the similar species *Camellia lutchuensis*. In addition, there are many readily available japonica hybrid camellias that are fragrant.

If you would like to add a little fragrance to your winter garden, here is a list of recommended varieties. Bear in mind this represents only a partial selection and research is ongoing to increase the number of fragrant hybrids. So the options will surely expand. Check with your local club or nursery and keep an eye on the camellia literature for new "scentsations" appearing on the market.

Fragrant Camellias	
Ack-scent	Herme
Apple Blossom	High Fragrance
Cara Mia	Kramer's Supreme
Cinnamon Cindy	Scentsation
Erin Farmer	Scentuous
Fragrant Pink	Sweet Emily Kate

Cold Hardy Camellias

Camellias need a certain amount of cold weather to bloom, so don't fret when the mercury heads south. While a perfect camellia climate is warm humid summers in the 80s, followed by gentle cool nights in the 30s, camellias can withstand more extremes of heat and cold. Such colder temperatures are even *necessary* for certain varieties to bloom properly.

In the "Camellia Belt", a sudden cold snap may damage a few flowers and mature buds that are nearly open, but the immature buds will still bloom when normal temperatures return. In colder climates, it may be necessary to plant the camellia under high cover, such as a tall evergreen (pines are ideal) or an artificial structure. A southern exposure, shielded from the cold north wind by a hedge or wall may also work. Microclimates also play a role, such as low spots that collect colder air. Some say that plants in sunny locations tend to have deeper roots, which promotes cold hardiness.

The trouble really starts when the mercury dips below 10° F. The greatest risk of plant damage is during either a very sudden or very prolonged deep freeze, when certain camellia species (except selected cultivars) begin to suffer tissue damage, especially below 5° F. While camellias can handle that range if the cool-down is gradual, a sudden cold blast followed by a quick warming may cause the bark to split. Therefore, in a colder climate such as New York or New Jersey, it may be wise to consider the newer hybrids bred especially for cold hardiness. Many of these hybrids have been field tested as far north as USDA Zone 6.

Even within the japonica family there are certain varieties that are proven hardy to Zone 7. While the genetic makeup of these japonicas has enabled them to better survive freezing weather, there is a wide variety of japonicas and hybrids that are bred to withstand temperatures in the 0° F range and below. Some may occasionally experience bud damage during extreme cold weather and thus may benefit from a protected location. Nevertheless, the plants have proven hardy after a number of years of testing at various sites in the northeast to temperatures as low as -10° F.

The late Dr. William Ackerman of Ashton, Maryland (a former U.S.D.A. plant breeder with the U.S. National Arboretum) and Dr. Clifford Parks, a botanist in North Carolina, have developed a number of cold hardy camellias. Here is a partial list of both Fall-blooming and Spring-blooming cold hardy varieties.

Fall Blooming Cold Hardy Varieties

These will do well in Zone 6b and possibly 6a in protected locations. Generally, they will bloom in mid-fall and can

Fall Blooming Cold Hardy Varieties	
Ashton's Pride	Winter's Dream
Lushan Snow	Winter's Fire
Mason Farm	Winter's Hope
Polar Ice	Winter's Interlude

Survivor	Winter's Rose
Snow Flurry	Winter's Star
Winter's Beauty	Winter's Waterlily
Winter's Charm	

Spring Blooming Cold Hardy Varieties

These will do well in Zone 6b and possibly 6a although some shelter or protection is suggested. Generally, these bloom in April.

Spring Blooming Japonicas and Hybrids	
April Blush	Fire 'n' Ice
April Dawn	Ice Follies
April Kiss	Jerry Hill
April Remembered	Pink Icicle
April Rose	Spring Icicle
Betty Sette	

A lengthier list of cold hardy camellias is available from the American Camellia Society, either on its website or from many local ACS-affiliated clubs. Nurseries in colder regions are also a good resource.

Sun-Tolerant Camellias

Camellias do need plenty of sunlight to grow and bloom properly. It is a common misconception that camellias are "shade" plants that cannot be grown in sun. Yes, as native understory plants, they are more tolerant of shade than most plants, and they generally will survive in shade. However, the fact is a camellia can and must have as much sunlight in all regions as possible without injury. Sunshine produces not only a more vigorous plant; it also promotes blooms that are better in quantity and quality. The sun's heat likewise promotes larger blooms.

In locations with intense summer heat, wind, or drought, it is wise to provide some shade protection, but not too much. Too much shade produces leggy foliage, sparse blooms, and less disease resistance. Morning sun combined with afternoon shade, or continuous half sun under dappled tree shade, is ideal. Even in sunny spots, most camellias will do well if they are properly planted, well mulched, and receive enough water (at least an inch per week).

In areas with very humid summers, camellias can be grown even in full sun. A doubting Thomas need only visit a nursery that produces field-grown camellias like row crops in full sun, or travel country roads where giant camellias stand fully exposed around farmhouses. Camellias have been grown like that for generations, and they grow more quickly and vigorously than in shade. Field-grown camellias, where available, are strong enough to withstand being dug, balled, and transplanted in virtually any garden location.

Several "can't miss" sun-tolerant camellias are widely available and commonly grown in many regions:

Sun Tolerant Camellias	
Daikagura	Governor Mouton
Debutante	Herme
Don Mac	Jarvis Red
Dr. Tinsley	Kramer's Supreme
Kumasaka	Professor Sargent
Lady Clare	Rose Dawn
Leucantha	Rosea Superba
Marjorie Magnificent	R.L. Wheeler
Pink Perfection	Sasanqua (all)

The newer *Camellia reticulata* hybrids also perform well in full sun. These camellias produce the largest blooms – some over 6 inches wide – in vibrant colors that amaze visitors (and judges) at camellia shows. While they generally are more tender and cold sensitive than japonica, many new reticulata hybrids have a sufficient amount of japonica DNA to be relatively hardy outdoors in the warmer regions of the Camellia Belt. In fact some have been around long enough to have a proven track record outside.

Here is a list of popular *Camellia reticulata* hybrids that have the potential to be successfully grown outdoors in regions with very mild winters:

Fall Blooming Cold Hardy Varieties	
Dr. Clifford Parks	Lauren Tudor
Frank Houser	Larry Piet
Francie L	Phyllis Hunt
Harold Paige	Ray Gentry
Hulyn Smith	Ruta Hagman
Linda Carol	Valentine's Day

Some final caveats are appropriate regarding camellias planted in full sun. First is the importance of humidity in the sun tolerance of a camellia. In dryer climates, a camellia in full summer sun may need daily irrigation as well as sprinkling of the foliage in late afternoons to replace the water loss and maintain strength, especially as the plant is budding. Second, if camellias are planted in a dry sunny location with no irrigation, it is wise to start small. A smaller plant stands a better chance of surviving dry conditions than a larger one, as it needs less water while getting established. Such plants should also be mulched heavily to retain soil moisture. Third, for larger plants, it is best not to plant a greenhouse-grown camellia in full sun immediately. Gradual acclimation is helpful for the same reason that people get sunburned in spring. And finally, be mindful that the root system of a greenhouse-grown camellia may not be as adapted to full sun, so keep an eye on the moisture level.

 # Cold Climate Planting

Although many exciting new hybrids are dispelling the myth that camellias cannot be grown in cold climates (north to Zone 6), the northern gardener does have a different set of rules for planting camellias. In northern climates, for instance, planting in late fall can be disastrous.

The best time for planting camellias in the north is late spring, preferably April and May, after the ground has thawed. The best location is a north or western exposure, sheltered from cold winds. A higher elevation is better than a frost pocket that gathers cold air; and when planting on slopes choose the top rather than the bottom. All other recommendations about planting in Chapter 8 apply here, such as "planting high" in a spot with slightly acidic soil that is well drained.

An excellent resource for northern gardeners is the book *Growing Camellias in Cold Climates* by Dr. William L. Ackerman. A long-time Maryland resident and former Director of Research at the U.S. National Arboretum, Dr. Ackerman was a pioneer in developing cold-hardy hybrids. Here is his summary of planting instructions.

Dr. Ackerman's *Summary for Northern Gardeners*
1. Plant in spring rather than fall, and water well

the first two years.

2. Avoid full sun by planting under an over-story tree if possible.
3. Select a northern or western exposure, with protection from winter winds.
4. Choose a location with slightly acid, well-drained

Landscape Camellias

More than a Pretty Bloom

It has been said that the camellia, as a landscape plant, is "imprisoned by its own blooms." We are so captivated by its blooms we often don't fully appreciate the handsome plant behind it! This problem is really psychological, as the camellia (above any other ornamental) possesses extremely attractive foliage year round, lending an elegant presence. Even if camellias never flowered, they should be ranked high on the list of desirable landscape plants.

How fortunate is the person who acquires a property with old camellias and recognizes their great worth. A collection of old camellias may easily serve as the centerpiece of a garden landscape, even if they need shaping up. Few property owners will ever be able to own a mature camellia without transplanting mature specimens from elsewhere, which some do (at considerable expense)!

There once was a time in the early 1900s when large camellias were so rare that nurserymen in the coastal south searched everywhere to find them, and purchased them at great prices for shipping by railcar to large estates in cities like Atlanta, Charleston, and Richmond. Then, and even now, a mature camellia is a valuable feature adding richness to any landscape, and is well worth saving.

In fact, if the camellia were never discovered, botanists

would be hard pressed to find a single plant that combines the qualities of a sturdy evergreen shrub that is elegant and tidy in appearance, low in maintenance, drought resistant, and tolerant of virtually all weather conditions. Its various shapes make it ideal for use as hedges (short or tall), specimen plants, group plantings, understory trees, topiary standards, and even container plants.

A little known fact is that camellias live for centuries -- longer even than the South's treasured Live Oaks. Some of the world's oldest camellia plants, more than a thousand years old, still stand in temple gardens in their native Asia. It is amazing to think that your new camellia may become tomorrow's heirloom, perhaps living beyond the year 3,000!

The camellia's heartwood is packed with carbon and consequently so dense, heavy, and strong that it was used as charcoal by Asian cultures. Its seeds were crushed as a source of seed oil (similar to olive oil) for cooking and lighting. The species *Camellia oleifera* from which the word "oleo" was derived (although the butter substitute never contained any oleifera oil) is again grown as a commercial seed crop in the U. S.

The camellia's leaves, specifically *Camellia sinensis*, have been a source of tea as far back as 2700 B.C., and they are the reason camellias were introduced to Europe and America in the first place. What an irony – that the camellia originally was imported *not* for its blooms but for its foliage! And yet the landscape use of camellias has scarcely been explored.

The camellia is outstanding as a foliage plant in almost any setting. Because of its varied growth habits, camellia plants can be successfully used as accent specimens, standards and pillar shapes (such as for entrances), basic "foundation" shrub plants, hedges, espalier, and woodland garden group plantings.

Camellia Landscape Plants -- Why So Rare?

So why are camellias now rarely seen in modern residential landscapes when once they were so popular and still are resplendent in older neighborhoods? It is because of the boom in residential subdivisions, which produced a great demand by contractors for "instant" landscapes. That demand was met by commercial production of fast growing foliage plants that can be produced and sold quicker and cheaper. Landscape installers on a fixed budget liked the cheap plants, which offered more "green" for the buck. They winked at the reality that fast growing substitutes tend to be short-lived and grow like weeds -- requiring almost constant pruning and maintenance (at the homeowner's expense).

Quite frankly, camellias, because of their diverse growing habits, are highly suitable for residential landscapes. This diversity is what makes them amenable to so many different uses. Consider that camellias generally fall into five different growth habits: upright and spreading, upright and columnar, rounded and compact, irregular and spreading, and compact and low growing.

For tall or short hedges, camellias are particularly well-suited – especially *Camellia sasanqua*, a vigorous, fast-growing, free-blooming species that is ideal. Sasanquas bloom in waves during autumn, and they can withstand more sun, heat, cold, drought, rain, neglect and mass trimming than nearly any other landscape plant. With their fragrant blooms and shiny evergreen foliage, they far surpass the more commonly used privets, ligustrums, hollies, boxwoods, and pittosporums that are often seen. And with much more class!

Collector's Landscape

For many camellia growers, a practical distinction can be made between "gardening" and "landscaping." Some growers select camellia plants solely with the objective of building a collection of many different varieties that they grow primarily for their blooms, which are harvested for cut flowers or camellia shows, or just to be enjoyed during blooming season.

For these gardeners, the primary considerations are access and proximity, which allow for grooming the plants and harvesting their flowers, not to mention the satisfaction of strolling and admiring the collection. These are specialty gardeners who love camellias and enjoy tending them year round, often displaying and sharing blooms that are the envy of the neighborhood. A guided visit to such a garden during peak bloom can be truly memorable.

Other equally camellia-centric gardeners want a more classic garden setting for their collection. A common practice is to plant camellias in large beds or patches within a larger garden, which otherwise contains traditional design features like pathways, fountains, and companion plants. The large camellia beds often contain specially amended soils and are defined by a border of stone, wood or low-growing plants.

Generalist's Landscape

If you have a professional landscape designer, you can leave to the experts the decision where to plant new camellias. In every other case, choosing the right location for a new camellia is a function of the effect you want to achieve. This process can benefit from some careful forethought.

If your property is a "blank slate" with no existing layout, a good starting point is to sketch a design with pleasing lines and gradual curves, behind which are planted camellias and other ornamentals (which may be added over time). You should resist the urge, described by one fellow gardener who is a self-described "plopper," to simply pick a random spot. Another practice to avoid is scattering camellias in an open lawn where they face the threat of competing grasses and string-trimmers, not to mention the major challenge of mowing around them. A group planting in a prepared bed is much easier on both the gardener and the plant.

If you have an existing landscape, the process of adding camellias may start by envisioning an "outdoor picture" of the garden with camellias added in various locations, like works of art. Where a location is identified, an appropriate variety may be paired – such as a specimen camellia in areas of high visibility versus a mass blooming variety for a background or screen. Camellias can easily be blended into a woodland setting as well, such as along the edge of a tree line, similar to their native habitat.

In choosing a location it is always important to consider certain basic aspects of camellia growth habits. As explained elsewhere in this book, the growth rate of camellias is directly proportional to the amount of available sunlight. As shade increases, growth decreases significantly. Thus certain varieties may be better suited for a particular location. A sasanqua, for instance, grows much faster than a japonica, especially in a sunny spot where its mass of flowers makes a stunning impression when seen from a distance. In contrast, the larger and more exquisite japonica blooms are much better appreciated close up in filtered sunlight.

The blooms of certain varieties should also be considered in picking a location. A beautiful white blooming variety, for instance, will be under-appreciated if planted against a light colored structure, whereas a contrasting red bloom will really stand out. A fragrant bloom is outstanding in high traffic areas, but its fragrance is lost when planted in a background. Many gardeners have a practice of selecting camellia varieties based on when they bloom and arranging them so the flowering season extends from early to late – "stretching the season" as we say -- from September until May.

Other Landscape Uses

When considering a specimen plant, choose the showiest variety available. For large and exquisite single blooms, an excellent choice would be 'Frank Houser,' 'Francie L,' 'Tomorrow Park Hill,' 'Edna Bass,' or 'Valentine's Day.' For maximum color impact, one might consider a large and highly floriferous sasanqua such as 'Stephanie Golden' or 'Leslie Ann.'

For foundation plantings (near the base of a structure) a low-growing sasanqua is much better than a boxwood or holly and it seldom needs pruning. Sasanquas always bloom heavily and require very little maintenance to hold their shape and height. 'Shi-shi gashira' (red) is a proven standout, as are 'Showa no sakae (soft pink), 'Reverend Ida' (hot pink), and 'Green's Blues' (red fading to a bluish shade).

For tall screens, a sasanqua will outshine a ligustrum any day, with 'Rose of Autumn' and 'Kanjiro' (both reds) growing fast and upright. Three other selections, nearly as vigorous, are 'Mine no yuki' (white), 'Leslie Ann' (white with pink edges), and 'Stephanie Golden' (hot pink). In recent years, nurseries have released many new fast-growing heavy-blooming sasanquas, so the above named varieties are merely suggestive.

Good companion plants will enhance your camellia collection, some of the best choices being hydrangeas (which bloom opposite camellias), hybrid azaleas, Japanese maples, crape myrtles, dogwoods, gardenias, citrus, and hollies. Take care to avoid planting anything that will grow very large and overshade the camellias. Nearly all perennials and annuals can be planted fronting camellias with good affect.

Period and Theme Gardens

Many camellia enthusiasts, depending on space available, have come to enjoy organizing their garden around a particular theme, and collecting camellias accordingly.

Examples are gardens that contain varieties with similar bloom characteristics such as color (all reds or whites), bloom forms (all formal doubles), or other features (fragrance, or newly discovered species).

Others enjoy preserving vintage historical camellias, especially if they have the good fortune of gardening on a property that dates to a certain period. These "period" gardens are like living museums, containing camellias that have historical significance. Such plants offer more than just a beautiful bloom; they have a pedigree or legend attached.

Some of the oldest camellia varieties, once thought lost to time, have been rediscovered in recent years, thanks to a group of modern sleuths who would make Sherlock Holmes proud. They combine 21st century technology with old-fashioned "gum shoe" investigative techniques to locate and propagate those varieties so modern camellia gardeners can have the best of the past and present.

Four Periods of Camellias

Camellia gardeners typically group plants into four periods representing distinct varieties of camellias dating to those periods.

Antique (Pre-World War I)

After commerce and religion introduced camellias to Europe from Asia in the 17th century, the Europeans' love for the plant peaked two hundred years later in the 1800s. Celebrated in art and literature during the Victorian period, the greatest nurseries in England, France, Belgium, and Italy cultivated the plant for its exceptional beauty. Many varieties introduced during that period were associated with, and named for, various members of royalty or noble benefactors.

Upon entering the U.S. in the early 1800s, camellias quickly captured the fancy of nurserymen and their customers who were able to afford gardens and conservatories. After the Civil War many rare ones were forgotten until interest reignited in the run up to World War I in the early 20th century.

Historical (World War I to 1949)

The renewed interest in camellias after World War I was met with a resurgence of the nursery industry, which began producing new varieties. Growers from the Southeast to the West Coast bred new plants from seed imported from Japan, which resulted in the availability of new varieties that joined the Antiques in American gardens. This was a period when nurseries became more industrialized, making plants more affordable for the middle class. Many of these plants still survive in abandoned nurseries and neglected public gardens, cemeteries, and estates, which serve as a testament to the camellia's rugged endurance.

Heirloom (1950 to 1959)

During the late 1950s, interest in camellias reached its zenith. Organizations such as the American Camellia Society (founded in 1945) were heavily promoting the camellia to gardeners across the nation who began forming local, state, and regional camellia associations. Specialized camellia gardens became such an attraction during the winter months that venues such as Bellingrath Gardens, which had accumulated one of the world's finest collections, needed traffic control during the peak blooming season.

Modern (1960 to Today)

The Modern period has witnessed the camellia's ups and downs since the peak of 1959, although it has abounded in producing more new varieties (including sensational hybrids) than any previous period. Today's gardens feature the newest colors alongside traditional favorites. Research and development continues to yield more colors, fragrance, cold hardiness, and other desirable characteristics which, thanks to technology, are more accessible and affordable than ever.

 ## Container Camellias

Camellias in handsome pots will enhance any garden or outdoor space and are a necessity if you live in an apartment or town home. However, they involve a little extra detail because of the artificially confined root zone.

Unlike in the open ground, which allows water run-off, good drainage is a matter of life and death for a potted camellia. Avoid heavy potting mixes that stay soggy when watered. Choose a growing medium with a heavy percentage of large porous particles, like crushed pine bark. Plant 1-2 inches below the rim, with only enough soil on top to cover exposed roots. A light mulch of pine straw or Spanish moss is attractive and will help prevent evaporation.

When planting only a few containers the best option is to use a premixed bag of "planting mix" from a garden center. These usually combine crushed bark, peat moss, compost, and other ingredients that supply nutrients and porosity. If mixing your own, a good recipe includes 3 parts crushed bark, 1 part peat moss, and ½ part perlite. One tablespoon of superphosphate per gallon of planting mix is optional to promote a healthy pH and improve root development.

Choose a container with large drain holes, which some growers cover with screen mesh to block insects. Container design is a matter of taste but should not be so decorative as to compete with the plant's beauty. Solid colors are best. Since drain holes are at the bottom, it is helpful to place the container on feet or pavers rather than bare ground.

Regular watering is important, especially during drought. Bear in mind that nutrients leach over time, so slow release fertilizers are widely used. Liquid fertilizers also are recommended. Place a potted camellia where it will receive adequate sunlight without getting so hot that it dries out quickly. One advantage of a potted camellia is portability, for finding that "just right" location!

Planting & Care
How Not to Kill a Camellia

It seems inconceivable, but is true, that today's new camellia may still be alive in the year 3,000! Yes, a well-established camellia is among the hardiest and longest living plants on earth. That is assuming we don't kill it ourselves first! As the focus shifts to planting and care, we have a true confession: every experienced camellia grower, without exception, is also experienced at killing them! The truth is, however, camellias are so easy to grow that this chapter might be more effective and amusing if it just listed "what not to do" from the mistakes we have made. Here is our list.

Common Ways to Kill a Camellia
Time-tested ways to injure or kill a camellia
• Plant too low
• Let the plant dry out
• Plant in a wet spot
• Spray with Roundup
• Set it on fire
• Pamper and Spoil it
• Cover with plastic during a freeze
• Apply pure nitrogen fertilizer
• Spray dormant oil in summer heat
• Acquire a new puppy who digs

Of course, the number one way to kill a camellia is with a bulldozer, which is 100 percent effective! Aside from that, it is no exaggeration to say that a mature camellia is nearly indestructible. They laugh at chainsaws, regenerating into handsome shrubs even stronger than before. They can survive epic droughts, floods, rockslides, hurricanes, and even ocean tsunamis. They are rugged enough – imagine this -- to survive for centuries without human care and attention!

This chapter is about how to give a camellia a good start, as well as how to avoid killing it by the second most lethal method: excessive pampering!

Planting – How, When, Where

Growing a good camellia starts with good planting. An old saying among veteran camellia growers is, "Never plant a fifty dollar camellia in a fifty-cent hole!" Thankfully, most camellias no longer cost fifty dollars. But many gardeners do often buy a new plant and promptly make the common mistake (as we have) of not planting it properly. Planting a camellia is really quite easy. And if properly planted, it can withstand almost total neglect while blooming beautifully for generations to come. Camellias cannot, however, overcome poor planting.

The most important thing to know is that a camellia needs to be planted slightly high in relation to ground level. It is absolutely essential to get the planting depth right. The top of the root ball should rest slightly above grade (that is, don't bury it) leaving no new soil atop the

root ball. If the camellia is planted too low, or it later sinks below the ground level, it is doomed to a slow death while you are wondering why. It therefore is safer to err on the side of planting too high than too low. Be careful to dig the hole no deeper than the root ball, or alternatively tamp down the bottom firmly, so the plant does not later sink.

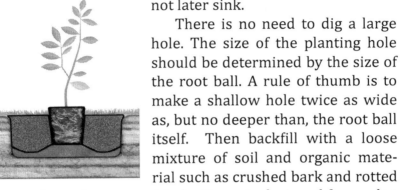

There is no need to dig a large hole. The size of the planting hole should be determined by the size of the root ball. A rule of thumb is to make a shallow hole twice as wide as, but no deeper than, the root ball itself. Then backfill with a loose mixture of soil and organic material such as crushed bark and rotted leaves. A good commercial planting mix designed for garden shrubs can also be used.

Upon removing a plant from the container, loosen the roots including any fine roots that may be bound tightly around the outside. This can be done by hand, or with a garden tool. To the extent you can spread any roots the plant will benefit. Once the camellia is placed in the hole, backfill with the amended soil. Then firmly pack the soil around the root ball by hand to remove any air pockets. Check again to be sure the top of the plant – now firmly planted – is still slightly above ground level. Overlay this with some light mulch, such as pine straw or

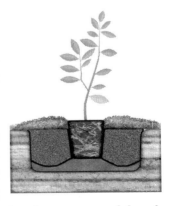

oak leaves.

As soon as the new camellia is planted, water it well for several minutes (saturation) by hose. Then wait a few days before the next watering to do it again. A newly planted camellia should be watered regularly the first year and given a good soaking anytime the soil shows signs of drying out. Watering deeply once a week, as with a soaker hose, is more beneficial than frequent shallow watering. A newly planted camellia should never be allowed to dry out during the first year (which will produce leaf wilt, then defoliation).

Finally, before you forget, tie on a label with the camellia's variety name. If it came with a plastic nametag that may be unnecessary at first, as most plastic labels last a few years. The best labels are metal tags with the name etched or written in permanent ink. It also is wise to make a written record and keep track of your camellias by name. Knowing the name will help you appreciate it more, as you will be able to read about it and share the name with admiring visitors when they ask. It also may be helpful to have a record of the variety name in case the need arises regarding its specific care and needs.

Special Planting Situations

The above instructions, which assume a flat, reasonably well-drained location, are a general guide as to which there are some important exceptions. It the ground is sloped, there is no need for the root ball to be planted high, but it must be slightly "heeled in" to grow upright. Good drainage is no problem because of the slope, and high planting may actually result in erosion of the root ball, exposing some roots. Even in flat terrain, if the soil is extremely dry and un-irrigated, more depth can be beneficial (albeit still slightly above grade) to better retain moisture in the hottest months.

Conversely, in a low-lying situation near the water table, one may need to plant camellias much higher in a raised bed or berm. Growers in places like Slidell, Louisiana (a "Camellia City") often plant virtually on top of the ground, digging only a shallow hole to promote plant stability and drainage. They then mound the soil around it or plant several camellias to-gether in a raised bed.

A common saying is, "camel-lias can't stand wet feet," and the proper planting height may require that it be high enough to keep the camellia roots from standing in wet soil.

In warmer regions of the Camellia Belt the best time to plant is generally fall after a plant has gone dormant -- ide-ally November to January. This allows time for the roots to adjust and grow before hot weather arrives. If not possible to plant in fall, it can still be done in early spring, which has the added advantage of allowing one to purchase plants that have been observed in bloom.

In northern regions, Dr. Ackerman has recommended that camellias be planted in spring, after the ground is ful-ly thawed. Northern summers are relatively mild and thus summer heat is less a factor, making spring a better time to plant so the new camellia can get established before winter.

As discussed in a previous chapter, camellias can be planted almost anywhere, but certain locations are better. Their growth is much faster in sunlight, but camellias can be planted in shade, even heavy shade. The ideal location is one with dappled sunlight, such as under a high canopy of tall pine trees.

It is best to avoid planting camellias too near trees with aggressive surface roots (such as magnolias, oaks and certain crape myrtles), which quickly invade the root zone and compete for water and nutrients.

Camellias can be planted near a dwelling or wall, provided it is far enough away for ventilation and to accommodate future growth. Bear in mind that some camellias grow into small trees if left unpruned. Around masonry structures, one should take care to amend the soil or at least remove any remnants of concrete (lime) from construction. Camellias prefer acid soil conditions, and lime has the opposite effect.

Soil and Fertilizer

Soil quality is important in the growth of new camellias. Yes, wild camellias have been seen growing from rocky outcroppings along the slopes of coastal China and Japan, but don't try that at home! That is not the norm, and those camellias probably began life in shallow soil that eroded. Camellias do best in rich organic soil that is slightly acidic. These conditions are also best for azaleas and hydrangeas, which generally grow well in the natural soils of the "Camellia Belt." If you have any of those plants, you can almost certainly grow camellias with little or no soil amendment.

Depending on the particular site, especially if it ever has been excavated, the soil may need some amendment. There are many good "planting mixes" available at nurseries and home centers, or you can make your own. All have copious amounts of organic material or compost. For homemade mixes, it is recommended you include aged crushed pine bark (nickel sized nuggets), and organic matter such as rotted oak leaves, and peat moss. These materials can be mixed with topsoil or sand from the planting hole. Soil texture is equally important, as camellia roots grow best in loose, well-drained soil.

As a general rule a camellia should only be lightly fertilized the first year. The same is true for transplanted camellias. The reason is that nitrogen in fertilizer stimulates leaf growth, which makes the top grow before the roots have become well enough established to support the new growth. Too many new leaves plus not enough roots equal dead or stressed plants, especially in hot weather. Because root growth is very important at first, however, an application of Triple Superphosphate in the planting hole will help. This promotes root growth during the first year and can be purchased at most garden centers.

After a new camellia is established, spring is the best time to fertilize. Apply the fertilizer around the time the camellia is nearing its flush of new growth. As a rule of thumb, camellias should receive a good balanced fertilizer, spread around the drip line, in March and May. A slow-release, camellia-azalea fertilizer is a good choice that is formulated for acid loving plants. Some growers also use cottonseed meal, which is a good organic source of nitrogen that decomposes and releases slowly. Around late September some growers apply a light treatment of low nitrogen fertilizer, but this is optional.

Fresh mulch is highly recommended each spring and fall. Mulch helps the roots stay cool in summer, warm in winter, and retains moisture in the root zone. It also prevents erosion and weed growth. Most mulch materials can be used but most growers on the Gulf Coast prefer pine straw. It does not pack down or shed water as do many other mulches. A layer of 1-3 inches of pine straw once or twice per year is sufficient.

Pruning and Maintenance

As camellias get established, the process of keeping them in shape by trimming various parts is an activity that is almost entirely optional. One of the best things about camellias is that they do not require frequent pruning, unlike the fast growing and less desirable non-flowering shrubs that are so overused in most landscapes. The only real need for pruning is to reduce the size of an overgrown or leggy plant, to maintain a certain shape, or to control disease (such as twig blight). One big no-no is to avoid major pruning after spring unless you don't mind eliminating next year's flower buds. Another is to never prune camellias with hedge shears.

A fact to bear in mind while pruning is that certain varieties have different growth habits. Some are slower growers, thus producing much less stem growth annually. For example, if you prune a 12-inch length from a young 'Daikagura' or 'Magnoliaeflora' (slow growers) it may take at least two years for them to grow back. Other varieties such as 'Drama Girl' can produce 12 inches of new growth in a single year.

Where major pruning or restoration is necessary, you will be glad to know that camellias can take it. They can be cut back as far as necessary, even to a low stump, and still regenerate into a beautiful plant. The best time for this kind of pruning is when the plant is dormant when its energy is stored in the lower trunk and roots. It may take 1-2 years for the plant to resume producing blooms. But they will be better and larger than the leggy old plant of yore. A good fertilization in spring will help it rebound quicker.

Harvesting flowers is actually a form of pruning, and you

70

should not hesitate to take plenty of branch from a mature plant when cutting blooms for indoor enjoyment. A longer branch actually helps prolong a cut bloom when displayed in a vase, and the plant itself benefits from the light haircut. If your plant is very small, however, you may want to just twist the bloom off (float in water) so the growth bud is not cut off.

Another form of pruning is disbudding, which creates fewer but larger flowers. A reason for disbudding may be to enhance the plant's flower display or to produce more specimen blooms for cutting. The best time to disbud is early to mid-fall, once the buds are maturing and clearly visible. The process is easy, by simply twisting off the flower bud. It is beneficial to remove all buds from the interior of a plant, where the flowers will be unseen anyway. If a goal is to extend the plant's blooming period, you should leave some of both large and small buds. If the goal is to produce show-quality blooms, you should remove all buds on every stem, leaving only the terminal (tip end) bloom buds.

Transplanting Camellias

A camellia can be moved when necessary, with a couple of options depending on its size. The optimal time is winter or late summer while the plant is dormant.

A small camellia is easy to dig and move, needing only a shovel and wheelbarrow. A large plant requires careful planning. One option is a professional landscaper with a shrub spade, which obviously is ideal.

If doing it yourself, the goal is to keep as much root ball intact as possible. You probably will have to dig deeply around the trunk, cutting some thick feeder roots. It is wise to "root prune" the plant months ahead if possible, using a long sharp shovel on opposite sides of the plant approximately 8 and 6 months in advance.

The day before moving, water the plant deeply. Dig and move it quickly to minimize exposure. Once freed from the ground, the plant can be lifted onto a canvas tarp and dragged to a new location. The new planting hole (prepared in advance) should be slightly wider, but no deeper, than the root ball of the transplant. Be sure the transplant rests firmly on the bottom with its crown slightly above ground level.

Back fill with a good soil mix (i.e., large amounts of crushed bark and composted manure) to encourage new root growth. Fill any open holes with soil mix, watering well and tamping down to eliminate air pockets. Mulch well and soak the entire root zone, repeating every 2-3 days for two weeks. A transplanted camellia should then be watered regularly (including its foliage) until it beomes established.

 Did You Know?

People are the greatest natural enemy of mature camellias. While established camellias will often live for hundreds of years with little or no care, they are susceptible to bulldozers. Priceless collections have been lost to unknowing developers, who could have sold mature plants for hundreds or thousands of dollars. The lesson here is that camellia gardeners should keep their eyes open for these overlooked treasurers.

Enjoying Camellia Blooms

Floral Dividends

Walter Bellingrath, an early investor in Coca-Cola stock, knew something about dividends. He once wrote, after an enjoyable day in his magnificent Bellingrath Gardens, that he was "convinced the camellia has *no equal* in the plant world for its beauty and fitness for the beautification of the home and landscape." He was enjoying his camellia dividends!

Bellingrath Gardens, poised overlooking a bend in Fowl River near its entrance into Mobile Bay, is an outdoor stage for camellias, where they are enjoyed not just in the garden. Inside the stately home (as featured in the *America's Castles* television series) is a butler's pantry where Mrs. B. stored her elegant display pieces, still in use, for exhibiting blooms to admiring guests. The Bellingraths had so much fun they invited the entire public out to see!

The double-barreled display of camellia blooms, both indoors and out, brought out the state patrol! Traffic control was necessary to manage the massive crowds who streamed in by automobile. America was enjoying a perfect marriage of coincidence between cars and camellias. Bellingrath Gardens has since been open to the public seven days a week.

The same scene was unfolding in towns like the coastal village of Amelia Island, Florida (near Jacksonville). On a single weekend, a one-man outdoor camellia show hosted by the renowned Gus Gerbing drew over 40,000 souls to witness the spectacle of thousands of cut camellia blooms on display under moss-draped oaks along the St. Johns River. The public response inspired Gerbing to publish one of the first colorized camellia books depicting varieties of camellia blooms.

At Bellingrath Gardens, camellias were displayed in every possible setting. Its owner once found himself sharing advice with a visitor on how to best appreciate camellia blooms: "Stand back and view the overall display of the single bush. Then approach a single blossom and take it gently in your hand for study. Look at the petals – their perfect formation, and contemplate on your Creator's handiwork!" Good advice to this day.

One treat of growing camellias is having plenty of fresh cut flowers in January! The peak blooming season is during the middle of winter, when gardens are bare and the weather is cloudy and gray. For generations camellias have added color and class to our winter gardens, as well as warmth and beauty to our homes during the festive holiday season. The personal satisfaction of cutting and enjoying camellia blooms is addictive, not to mention they are lovely to share.

Cutting and Displaying Camellias

Camellias are nocturnal bloomers, their buds opening in darkness. So cutting fresh flowers is best done in early morning when they are newly opened. And don't be shy about cutting camellia blooms. A longer branch helps extend the life of a cut bloom indoors as displayed in a vase. The plant itself even benefits from the resulting light pruning. A large flat basket or tray is ideal for laying the blooms, facing upward, as they are collected. Handle the blooms gently after cutting or they may bruise.

Once inside, fresh camellia blooms should immediately be prepared for display. Make a fresh cut on the stem. Some growers crush the end to promote better water absorption, using a pair of pliers, or even strong teeth! Place the blooms in a bud vase, or a small cup or bloom vase. Fresh water is fine, although some people add a preservative such as Floralife. There are many home recipes for making floral preservatives with ingredients such as Sprite, bleach, or sugar.

An old technique for displaying camellias is to float the blooms in an attractive bowl of water. They also may be used effectively in flower arrangements, stacked in a tiered dish as a centerpiece, or even assembled dramatically in a simple pile. The different ways to display cut camellia blooms is limited only by the gardener's creativity.

For flower arranging, japonicas are the best blooms to use because as they hold longer than sasanquas and are lighter than the large reticulata blooms. To prevent blooms from dropping off the stem, floral wire can be used to secure the blooms to the stem by inserting the wire through the calyx (where the bloom attaches to the stem) and twisting it back around the stem.

Sasanquas can be used attractively in sprays by placing a blooming sasanqua limb in a large vase or arrangement. These sprays can be very impressive for a special occasion, but they generally last only a couple of days, depending on the freshness of the blooms and buds. Although some sasanqua blooms may shatter after the first day, the remaining buds often will still open.

A trick for extending the life of cut camellia flowers is to store them overnight in a refrigerator, removing them during the day or evening. In the refrigerator they should be stored dry in a sealed plastic container with a tight lid, layering the bottom with cotton or fiberfill as a cushion. A small amount of water in the bottom of the container will add just enough humidity to keep the bloom fresh. Spritzing the bloom with water when removed from the refrigerating helps promote freshness. If the container is not covered and sealed tightly in the refrigerator, the flower will often turn brown.

Some camellia growers spray chemical treatments on a bloom to preserve its freshness for several days. It works like a hair spray, sealing the moisture of the petals for a longer bloom life. This is a common practice among show exhibitors who often cut and store their blooms up to a week in advance. Such products are available from floral supply houses under commercial names like "Clear Set" and "Clear Life." Various homemade concoctions exist, such as Napthalene Acid discussed in the 1967 *American Camellia Yearbook*.

Another fun and interesting technique for displaying camellia blooms is to "wax" them by dipping a blossom in a warm mixture of paraffin wax and mineral oil. The effect can be stunning, producing a porcelain-like flower that hardly seems real. The waxed flower also lasts longer (requiring no water) because its natural moisture is sealed by the wax. The simple steps for this technique are described in Chapter 14. Waxed camellias are ideal for sharing with others, particularly shut-ins who can enjoy them on a bedside table.

Cutting Camellia Blooms
Cut blooms in the morning.
Take plenty of stem as needed.

> Avoid bruising the bloom when handling.
> Make a fresh stem cut and crush the end.
> Put bloom in a vase, water pick, or arrangement.
> Use fresh water or flower preservative.

Camellia Show Displays

One of the great traditions of the gardening world, dating to Boston in 1834, is to visit a local camellia show. You will see literally thousands of examples of the finest and most impressive specimens of camellia blooms, most of them grown in local gardens. It is an unforgettable sight!

There is no better place than a camellia show to get ideas for new varieties for your garden, plus advice and contacts about growing camellias. Some shows offer public clinics on subjects such as grafting, and many host a plant sale where you can find many rare and outstanding varieties on display at the show. These events are essentially conventions geared for everyone from the "merely curious" to the hardcore specialist.

Besides seeing perfect blooms, visitors to a camellia show can also see various camellia arrangements from simple groupings to more elaborate mixed arrangements. Some shows have a competition for sprays of blooming camellias, and even entire plants. Others may have an exhibit or competition for flower arrangements using camellias. A host club will often team up with other garden groups, such as Ikebana, to enhance the show.

At some point, even you may decide to enter some blooms in a show, which is easy and fun. Few things are more satisfying than seeing a bloom from your garden win a blue ribbon or trophy, making your plant forevermore a source of greater pride.

77

There is a special category for "novice" growers who have never entered a camellia show and may want some help.

Here are the simple basics for your first camellia show.

1. Arrive on time during the hours announced for entry of blooms (generally Saturday morning).

2. Bring some (even just one) of your best blooms cut that morning or the night before. Lay them on a tray for transport, the ends of their stems wrapped in a small piece of wet paper towel.

3. At the show entrance you will fill out a simple entry card for each bloom, listing the variety name. If you don't know its name, don't worry; someone will help you.

4. Place the bloom in a small cup of water (provided) and give it to a show clerk who will place it in the proper section -- for example the "novice" division.

5. Check back after the judging is over and claim your trophy or ribbon! Did someone mention floral dividends??

It is so easy -- that is all there is to it! Yes, the veterans have a few little extra things they do when entering blooms, but that will come. Start simple!! That is what the novice division is all about.

 ## Judging the Perfect Camellia

Where can 'Bob Hope,' 'Queen Elizabeth II,' 'Willard Scott,' and 'Elizabeth Arden' still be seen together in person?

Here is a clue. You are missing out if you have never visited a Camellia Show. It is the nearest thing to a celebrity gathering in the garden world. All across the nation, for nearly a century, shows have been held from November through March in peak camellia blooming season.

During weekend football clashes between X's and O's a competition of equal intensity (albeit more courteous!) is held for world-class camellia blooms, all grown by the home team – gardeners in your area. These are floral fireworks displays of unimaginable beauty where you will find hundreds of "must have" camellia varieties for your garden.

How is it possible to declare one camellia bloom better than another? This is where judges come in. Unlike zebra-shirted referees, camellia judges are fellow gardeners who have attended some training. Anyone can sign up for a 1-day program on camellia judging led by some of the world's experts. Even if you never intend to judge a camellia show, the experience is very worthwhile. You will learn all about the many camellia varieties, including which ones are rare, and what qualities make a perfect flower.

You may even decide to give judging a try. A nice benefit of judging is the privilege of being first to see the blooms at their peak freshness and hear the other judges' evaluations before the show opens to the public. And the fellowship of rubbing shoulders with experts is a great experience.

New judges serve an apprenticeship of at least 2 years before they advance as ACS Accredited Judges. They then are eligible to be invited to judge shows on the regional and national level -- a great honor for any camellia gardener.

If you are interested in attending a judges seminar, details are on the ACS website at www.AmericanCamellias.org.

Did You Know?

Massee Lane Gardens in Fort Valley, Georgia (near Columbus) is the official headquarters of the American Camellia Society. The gardens, featuring thousands of camellias are open to the public.

Camellias were first reported on the Gulf Coast in 1839 when a gentleman named Gilbert Rotton settled in Mobile, Alabama with about 50 varieties.

In 1953, in the Mobile area alone, there were not thousands but millions of own-root camellias for sale.

All of these cities are known as the "Camellia City: Greenville, Alabama; Fresno, California, and Slidell, Louisiana.

The award-winning Camellia japonica 'Magic City' is named after the city of Birmingham, Alabama.

Camellias have been growing at Arlington (family home of Robert E. Lee) since before the civil war.

Gibberellic Acid

Fooling Mother Nature

Gibberellic Acid, commonly known as 'gib' (pronounced "jib"), is one of the great secrets of the camellia world. It is the answer to the mystery of how certain growers produce blooms twice as large as normal! It is also the way to induce early flower blooms from a variety whose normal bloom season is weeks later.

A tiny drop works like magic. It functions for camellias like a growth hormone, fooling Mother Nature into producing earlier (and larger) camellia blooms. Gibbed blooms are not only larger and earlier; they often are more vibrant and longer lasting whether cut or left on the plant.

Why Use Gib?

Any gardener can have fun gibbing a few camellia buds, even if only to experience the wonder of watching them burst into bloom long before normal. However, it can be addictive!

The early inducement of blooms is what makes gib most useful to camellia growers, especially in regions where cold weather arrives sooner. Gib-induced blooms can beat the freeze and also be timed ahead of petal blight, which attacks many mid-season flowers in warmer climates. Gib makes the treated blooms larger and brighter in color, an asset to both casual gardeners and show exhibitors. The overall benefit is that gib allows you to essentially "pre-order" some nice blooms early in the season, even while sasanquas are still in bloom, ideal for autumn football and major holidays.

Another advantage of gibberellic acid is that it enables certain camellia shows to be held earlier in the season, well in advance of peak camellia blooming period. Such shows, often referred to as "gib shows," often feature a larger percentage of high quality blooms because they have been treated. For those lucky to visit or participate in one of the "gib shows," nothing ignites more excitement for the upcoming season. It is like baseball spring training for gardeners!

The advantage of gibbing, therefore, is that it induces earlier blooms before cold weather arrives and it lets a gardener schedule them to bloom around a particular event or holiday. Gibbed blooms also are generally larger and more beautiful than their untreated siblings. They will wow your neighbors and friends.

What a marvelous invention – how is it even possible?

Gibberellic acid is one of botany's all-time great accidental discoveries. It began in 1828 when a Japanese rice farmer, T. A. Konishi, had a problem with his rice seedlings. He noticed that certain seedlings were taller than others but they failed to produce any grain. For a rice farmer, this was a serious problem -- "no grain, no gain!" Konishi turned to science, but alas he never lived to see the mystery solved. It was not until the 1930s that researchers discovered that the symptoms found in Konishi's rice seedlings were caused by a previously unknown fungus. They were able to isolate the fungus and began to experiment on other plants, with surprising results.

Gib's effect on camellias was first reported in the late

1950s when experts in California announced that it induced rapid growth of flower buds, producing earlier, larger blooms. That news shot like lightening through the camellia world! Soon camellia growers everywhere were clamoring for it.

Gib -- When and How

The best time to use gib is beginning in September when flower buds are beginning to mature (growing round and plump). Select a well-developed flower bud. Twist and remove the growth bud immediately adjacent to the flower bud. The twisted-out growth bud will leave a small cup or wound next to the flower bud. Place a tiny drop of gib in the cup or wound where the growth bud was removed. That is all!

It is not necessary to apply more than a small drop of gib  to a flower bud. One small drop, applied with an eyedropper or syringe needle, is all it takes. Nature does the rest. As a popular hair-tonic ad once touted, "A little dab will do ya!"

It is considered a good practice to treat no more than a few buds per plant, es-  pecially on a smaller plant. After a gibbed flower is removed, it also is a good practice to prune back the branch to the next healthy growth bud. The reason is that no new growth will emerge from the treated end of the stem where the growth bud was removed.

Experienced growers, with years of using gib on camellias, report that it is not injurious to a mature healthy plant. However, it definitely is not a substitute for good plant care, and gib should be used only on healthy growing plants. It is not recommended for weak plants, or young plants having only a few flower buds, as too much gib may stress the plant.

The long-term effect of gib on plants is not fully known. Research cautions that where gib is used on over 50 percent of the buds, a plant may be weakened. It therefore is thought best not to gib a large percentage on any single plant. A rule of thumb is to gib no more than 10 to 15 percent of the buds in a season. It is also suggested that a few buds (no more than 3 to 4) be treated each week rather than all at once, so as to spread the blooming interval.

The time from bud treatment until a gibbed bloom opens is not predictable with exactness. The general time is 6-8 weeks, depending on the size of the bud and the variety. If gibbing for a certain event, many camellia growers set an advanced target of 45 days to begin gibbing buds every few days before and after the target date.

Several factors play a role in the bloom interval of a treated bud. Gib generally works better early in the season when the sap is still flowing and the plant is not completely dormant. Buds near the top of a plant generally respond quicker. Buds treated later in the season may not bloom any sooner than normal but may be slightly larger. The point is, the effect of gib decreases as dormancy increases.

Temperature and humidity are additional factors that may affect the interval, as are the overall health of the plant and the maturity of the bud at time of treatment. Dry days will slow the gib reaction, while humid days improve absorption, producing better results. Gib is also more effective when applied in the morning or late afternoon hours when temperatures are cooler and the bud is absorbing plant glucose.

For the above reasons, plants growing in a greenhouse (where temperatures remain mild and humid, postponing dormancy) generally respond better to gib than the same varieties grown outside where they go dormant quicker. The same effect is seen with outdoor plants in the mildest winter climates, such as gardens located at lower latitudes where gib remains effective until later in the season.

Some local camellia clubs create "gibbing calendars" that are calculated to show when buds should be treated based on a certain target date – such as the club's show. The Pensacola Camellia Club has an excellent one, and the 1981 *American Camellia Yearbook* contains instructions for making your own. Experimenters who want to investigate further uses of gib can find numerous articles published by the American Camellia Society and International Camellia Society.

Where to Find Gib?

Gibberellic acid is not expensive, but it is not carried by retail garden centers. It therefore can sometimes be a slight challenge to find a source.

Many local camellia clubs buy gib in quantity for distribution to club members for a small charge. It is mixed and ready to go, pre-packaged in eyedroppers that generally last an entire season. Unused portions, if refrigerated, are still effective the next year. Because the liquid is clear, some clubs and growers add some red coloring to their gib to make it easier to see when applying a small drop to a bud.

Gib also is available by order from nursery suppliers, either in person or online. It generally is sold under trade names like Pro-Gib or GibGro. For larger quantities, a liquid quart size of Pro-Gib generally costs around $50 and requires only mixing with 50 % water to create a 2% solution, which is ideal. Certain Internet vendors offer small kits under $20 which come in 5 gram quantities (eyedropper included) and require only mixing with alcohol or water per the seller's instructions.

Best Gibbed Varieties

Sixty years of experience has proven that gib has a highly beneficial effect on the buds of many varieties, but not all (oddly enough), as is discussed below. Here are a few varieties that respond well.

Japonica Varieties That Respond Well To Gibbing	
Adolphe Audusson	Junior Prom
Berenice Boddy	Kramer's Supreme
Buttons & Bows	Lady Clare
Clark Hubbs	Lady Laura
Daikagura	Leucantha
Debutante	Mansize
Dr. Clifford Parks	Marie Mackall
Dr. Tinsley	Mrs. Charles Cobb
Drama Girl	Morning Glow
Edna Bass	Nuccio's Jewel
Elizabeth Le Bey	Omega
Fashionata	Pink Perfection
Helen Bower	Rosea Superba
Governor Mouton	Royal Velvet
Grand Prix	Tiffany
Guilio Nuccio	Ville de Nantes
Julia France	

In addition to the list, gib also generally works well on all reticulata and retic hybrids, especially 'Dr. Clifford Parks,' 'Frank Houser,' 'Francie L,' 'Harold Paige,' 'Hulyn Smith,' 'Linda Carol,' 'Lauren Tudor,' 'Larry Piet,' 'Phyllis Hunt,' 'Ray Gentry,' 'Ruta Hagman,' and 'Valentines Day.'

The varieties that do not respond well tend to either suffer from bullnosing (causing the bud to not open fully and fall off) or the color becomes tinted or faded. Gib may work better for these varieties in other climates, so it is best to give it a try. Some less effective gib varieties may include 'Don Mac,' 'Finlandia,' 'Elegans,' 'Lallarook,' 'La Peppermint,' 'Margaret Davis,' 'Marjorie Magnificent,' 'Miss Charleston,' 'Nuccio's Gem', and many whites. Varieties such as 'Purple Dawn' and 'Professor Sargent' (both reds) may respond well in size but produce a blue tint.

 Did You Know?

Tea (the beverage, not the plant) was introduced to Europe in the middle 16th century. By the 1700s it began to replace beer as the beverage of choice at breakfast.

Did You Know?

- Gibberellic acid is sometimes used in the laboratory or greenhouse to encourage germination in otherwise dormant seeds.
- Gib is often used to increase fruit set. This results in more rapid growth of the fruit and fruit that may be partially or entirely seedless.
- Grape growers in particular use gib to boost production of grapes, especially Thompson seedless. The addition of gib encourages larger bundles and bigger grapes.
- Greenhouse tomatoes growers have also benefited from the effects of gib.

Camellia Propagation

Adventures in Camellia Growing

Why would a casual gardener be interested in methods of camellia propagation? Let's assume you are smitten with a rare camellia but it is not commercially available (and many are not). Or you want to expand your collection on a limited budget. Maybe you would like to duplicate a much-loved camellia from an ancestral home, but it is too large. You might even be one who likes to tinker and experiment. If any of these situations sounds familiar, this chapter is for you.

You may also yearn to create an entirely new camellia variety that you can name for someone in your family. The late Hulyn Smith, a former magistrate judge from Valdosta, Georgia, once said there is nothing like the thrill of walking out in the garden and finding a new variety blooming that only you and God have seen. Smith was well acquainted with that feeling, having produced some of the world's greatest new camellias. For most of us, that would be a "once in a lifetime" experience remembered forever.

As you may realize, the camellia is one of nature's "super plants" and there are few ways to experience them better than trying your hand at propagation. The methods are simple and worth a try, even for the amateur.

There are four main ways to propagate camellias. One is

"grafting" in which an existing camellia plant is cut down and a new variety is spliced onto its stump. Second is "air layering" in which a ring of bark is removed from a small limb that is wrapped in moss, forcing a new root ball to form around the ring, allowing the limb to be later cut off and potted as a new plant. Third is rooting cuttings, in which a small twig is removed and placed in a prepared rooting mix where it will sprout roots and grow. Fourth is planting seeds, which produces entirely new plants that bloom differently from either parent.

One of the best parts of camellia propagation is the hunt for a cutting from a certain variety you want to grow, which old-timers refer to as "trading wood." Cuttings and seeds are generally available free from other camellia enthusiasts, who are happy to share. It is this sharing and swapping of advice, techniques, "wood," and even tall tales, that adds to the camaraderie and satisfaction of growing camellias.

Grafting

The old cliché, "easier done than said," applies to grafting, the basics of which are simple. As with all propagation methods, timing is the key to success. The best time for grafting is when plants are completely dormant before the sap rises and new growth begins. In most "Camellia Belt" locations February (mid-winter) is ideal, plus or minus a few weeks. Once a graft is made, it takes about a month for the graft union to heal and form a callous before the newly grafted plant can start growing again on its borrowed roots.

Grafting materials and supplies are available around your house and at many stores. A plastic caddy is handy to hold everything. Here is what you will need.

Grafting Materials

- Very sharp knife that will stand up to being hit with a small hammer
- Small hammer
- Screwdriver preferably with a long shaft
- Coping saw with very small teeth
- Fungicide in a spray bottle
- Rubbing alcohol
- Rooting hormone – powdered
- Very small (artist –type) paintbrush for applying rooting hormone
- Florist tape, rubber bands, or twine for tying rootstock
- Single-edge razor blade
- Large cup or small trash can to cover graft

To get your graft off to a good start, it is essential to choose healthy, well-growing rootstock in a one or two-gallon pot. Most camellia gardeners prefer sasanqua for this purpose. Sasanqua is a vigorous growing species with a fibrous root system, which makes it ideal as a grafting rootstock. It also has a wider cambium layer (outer ring of bark) making grafting a little easier. There are some japonica varieties that also work well as rootstock, such as 'Professor Sargent,' and 'Governor Mouton,' but sasanqua generally works best and is widely available.

Another option is to graft on an older existing plant that is already planted in the ground. This is called "field grafting." It is ideal for older plants that need to be cut back anyway. It also can be done on root suckers or seedlings that have grown up from seed near an established plant. These cases offer a great opportunity to take advantage of a mature root system, which can make your grafts really take off.

Another source of rootstock is to make your own, by air layering sasanquas in your garden, as discussed later in this chapter. After a year or so in a pot, these air layers will have developed a root system and that allows the plant to be used as grafting stock.

Grafting Methods

There are many grafting techniques used by camellia growers, but the two most common methods are cleft grafting and high grafting. Both are fun and easy, even for a novice grower.

Cleft Grafting

Cleft grafting is by far the most popular method used by camellia growers. The process involves cutting off the rootstock to leave a short trunk, splitting the trunk, inserting the scion (cutting), covering it for protection, and waiting for the graft to heal and start growing. That's about it. Here is a more detailed description of those steps.

Preparing the Scion

Always use scions that are healthy. The best are those with several good "eyes" or growth buds. Careful inspection of a donor plant can sometimes yield scions with four or five eyes! Each of these eyes will sprout a branch on the new grafted plant. If you have the scions but can't graft them right away, no problem. Scions can be stored in a plastic bag in the refrigerator for several weeks (with just a tiny bit of water or damp paper towel for moisture).

To prepare the scion for grafting, you will need to trim the lower end for insertion into the cleft. An ideal scion should be about 2-3 inches long with two leaves remaining. Use a sharp knife or razor blade to whittle or trim the bottom of the scion to create a thin, tapered wedge. Make one side slightly wider than the other because you will be inserting the wedge-shaped scion into  the cleft along the outer edge of the rootstock. The wider side of the scion will match up with the outer (cambium) layer of the rootstock. The leaves of the scion should be cut in half to reduce the amount of leaf surface the stem will have to support while healing. Spray the entire scion with fungicide and set it aside while you prepare the rootstock.

Preparing the Rootstock

This step begins your plant surgery. Spray or wipe your knife, saw, and screwdriver with alcohol because the tools must be clean. Using a sharp saw with fine teeth, carefully saw off the rootstock leaving a stump 2-3 inches tall. (We like to cut it off a little high so if something goes wrong, there is enough rootstock to cut it back and try again.) Take extra care as you cut through to the opposite side of the trunk and slow down your sawing speed. That will help keep the cambium layer intact without tearing it. The goal will be to match the cambium layer of the rootstock with the cambium layer of your scion, so it heals and forms a calloused union. It is best to not use loppers or hand clippers for cutting back the rootstock, which often damages the cambium layer.

After you saw off the trunk, use a sharp knife to trim and

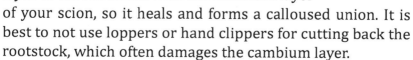

smooth the edges of the cambium layer around the cut surface. A special grafting knife is perfect, but any very sharp knife will work, as will a single-edge razor.

Next, place a large sharp knife across the center of the rootstock. Tap it carefully with a small hammer to split the rootstock about 1-inch down the stump. That will be far enough to pry open the split rootstock as you insert the scion. Before removing the knife from the cleft, insert a small thin screwdriver so it remains slightly open. Spray the opening lightly with fungicide.

Dip the scion in hormone powder and shake off the excess. As you hold the split rootstock slightly open, insert the scion. This is where extra care is needed. In order for the graft to "take" properly, the cambium layers of both the scion and the rootstock must line up exactly. This is the narrow layer of green bark on both. To help ensure good contact between the cambium layers, some grafting experts insert the scion at a very slight slant toward the center of the rootstock so the cambium layers are crossing.

Some people graft only one scion per trunk and others two – one on each side. You can experiment and see what works for you. We have grafted four to six scions on very large stumps. In those cases, where the stump is very large, you may need to insert small wedges in the cleft (a small nail is ideal) to alleviate some of the pressure of the large trunk so it does not crush the tender scion.

After you insert the scion, spray the graft lightly with fungicide. It may help to add some more hormone powder to promote a quicker graft union. For that task, a useful tool is a small artist's paintbrush partially cut off and stored in the container of hormone because it creates less waste than trying to sprinkle the powder on the graft. Lightly dab a little hormone around the graft union.

A final step is to tie florist's tape, rubber band, or twine around the rootstock at the point of the graft. This will ensure that pressure is maintained on the scion so it does not fall out from being too loose. Be careful not to disturb the scion after you carefully have lined it up with the cambium layer.

Finally, make a label for the newly grafted plant or write the variety name on the cover you use to seal the new graft. Then cover up the new graft, as described below.

Creating the Right Environment

A newly grafted scion needs a moist environment, but not too moist. One reason to spray it with fungicide at the time of grafting is to deter fungus that grows in wet conditions. How to create that sanitary environment is a subject of debate among grafters. The main point is to create an airtight covering for the new graft until it heals. The most common covering is a Styrofoam cup placed over the graft and sealed against airflow. This is an ideal cover if you are grafting onto a plant in a 1 or 2 gallon pot. To hold the cup in place and create a seal, add a layer of sand atop the potted rootstock where the cup or trashcan

will be resting. Make a ring in the sand and sink the cup into it so air cannot get in to the graft. A light sprinkling of water around the seal will promote air tightness.

Some grafters prefer other coverings, such as red plastic cups, small plastic trashcans, or plastic bags covered with newspaper. If you are making a field graft on an established plant in the garden, a small plastic trashcan works well. We have used several types of covering with success, depending on the size and location of the graft.

Caring for the Graft

After the major surgery is over, it is time to nurse the plant back to recovery. Keep the graft in a shaded location so it does not receive direct sunlight. If you grafted onto a potted rootstock, water it periodically just enough to keep the soil damp. Do not overwater, and avoid disturbing the airtight seal.

Patience is a virtue in grafting. Resist the urge to constantly peek at the graft to see if it is growing. Remember, you created a sanitary microclimate under the cup, and removing it risks introducing a contaminant. It is best to wait 3-4 weeks before lifting the cup to see how things are looking, but replace the cup promptly and reseal it.

Once the graft begins to produce new growth, you can punch a few small holes in the Styrofoam cup to introduce some air as it begins to "harden off." Eventually you will want to enlarge those air holes to a point when you can cut out the entire bottom of the cup, giving the graft some room for the new leaves to spread and grow. Once a callous has formed at the graft union, remove the tie or rubber band. If the rootstock has produced any shoots of its own, remove them.

If you discover your graft is wilting because of too many

air holes, seal it back up. The "hardening off" stage is very critical to the success of the graft. Too much air and sun (and resulting lack of moisture) will cause a graft to scorch and shrivel up. It is a good idea to keep the new graft shaded from any direct sunlight. A useful method is to use old political campaign yard signs, which can be moved easily to create shade.

Once your graft is hardened off and growing, you will be the proud owner of a new plant! This process may sound complicated at first, but the principle is simple and the technique gets much easier with practice. You will also develop your own techniques and preferences as you learn what works and gather tips from other growers.

High Graft

High grafting is a method of cleft grafting on the limbs of an established plant, well above ground. A graft can even be made on many branches at the same time. Some gardeners have been known to graft several different varieties on a single plant, thereby extending the blooming season for that plant. The record reportedly is held by W. F. Bailey of Orlando, Florida, who grafted 155 different varieties on a single 25-year old plant of 'Professor Sargent!'

The best time for high grafting is July to September when camellias are still growing but enter a period of late summer dormancy. (This may vary slightly by location and latitude.) The same tools and techniques for cleft grafting are used for high grafting: sawing off the limb, trimming the scion, splitting the branch, inserting the scion, and tying the branch.

The difference is, to cover the graft a 1 or 2-liter soda bottle is used, with the bottom cut out. After cutting out the bottom, first slide the bottle over the branch before you do the

graft. Once the graft is made, and the scion is in place, carefully slide the bottle back up to where the mouth covers the branch. Secure it into place with duct tape or electrical tape to make it firm.

Fill the mouth of the bottle with damp sphagnum moss. Then tape the bottom of the bottle back on. Make sure both the mouth and the bottom of the bottle are as air tight as possible. This will create a moist, protected microclimate for the tender graft. To protect it from sun, paint the bottle with white or light paint, or cover it with aluminum foil. If painting, leave a small place on the shady side so you can check the graft for progress. Use the same hardening off procedure as with cleft grafts. Gradually punch a few small holes in the bottle until the graft is hardened off and eventually the bottle is removed.

Air Layering

Air layering camellias is an ideal way to obtain a larger plant almost instantly. This process involves scraping away a ring of bark around a branch, wrapping the ring in sphagnum moss, then covering it with aluminum foil and waiting for a root ball to form in the moss. Nothing could be easier. This is a great method to use on plants that need pruning anyway after they have become overgrown or out of shape. Instead of cutting the branches off and throwing them away, an air layer can be made that will give you another plant.

The best time to make an air layer is spring when new growth begins and the plant's cambium layer is expanding. This results in a loosening of the bark, making it easy to scrape or peel away. Once the air layer is in place, the fact that the plant is in its growing season will result in faster development of roots.

Layering Materials	
• Sharp knife	• Sphagnum moss
• Small Pliers	• Heavy duty aluminum foil
• Hormone powder	• Twine or electrical tape
• Fungicide	• Survey tape
• Water bucket	• Ladder if working up high

Preparing the Moss

Soak the moss in a weak solution of fungicide and water in a bucket. Cut squares of foil about 12 inches square. You will need them big enough to wrap twice around a limb. If using twine, cut it to about 9 to 10 inches.

Preparing the Branch

Ideally choose a young branch with new growth. Older branches will take longer to form roots. Make sure there is  about 2 feet of branch above where the air layer is to be made. This will allow for a good-sized plant after it is removed from the original plant. With a sharp knife, cut or scrape away the bark of the limb to create a ring 1 ½ to 2 inches wide around the branch. If the ring is not wide enough, roots will not form. The bark can be scraped or peeled away with a knife, or using small pliers you can gently grind the bark away by twist the pliers

around it. The bark should come off easily. It is important to remove all bark from the ring or it will not form roots. Give the exposed ring a few extra scrapes to rough up the wood.

Now you are ready to enclose the ring in its new rooting environment. Dust the exposed ring with powered root hormone using an artist's brush. Take a handful of sphagnum moss and squeeze the water out, leaving it damp but not dripping wet.

Installing the moss is a technique that varies among different growers. The basic method is to wrap a fist-sized ball of dampened moss around the branch. (Hold the moss firm-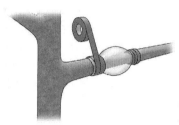ly in place with one hand, or the powder will rub off.) With your other hand, wrap the dampened moss with heavy-duty aluminum foil (dull side out). Then twist the ends of the foil around the limb to form a firm seal. Some growers also secure the ends with electrical tape, twine, or twist ties. It is important that an airtight environment is created.

The aluminum foil can sometimes attract pecking birds, even with the dull side out. A technique used by many growers is to spray paint the foil a green or dull color to avoid attracting birds.

Once you have the basic technique down, you may want to experiment with other enclosures besides aluminum foil. Some gardeners report good results with plastic cottage cheese or yogurt containers. A cut is made down the side of the container and across the bottom. A hole made in the bottom of the container that is approximately the same size as the branch, so it can be slipped around the branch. The container is then filled with potting mix or damp moss. The container lid is likewise cut across the top and a hole the size of the branch is cut in the middle. The lid is then snapped on around the limb and secured with duct tape so it remains sealed firmly in place.

Finally, once an air layer is made, flag the limb with survey tape so you will remember and be able to find it later.

Waiting for Roots

How long does it take for roots to form? Some air layers form roots in two to three months, whereas others can take longer. Much depends on the variety and how young the branch is. (Don't waste your time on an old branch or a very old plant.) After 2-3 months, gently squeeze the wrap. If roots are forming, it will feel slightly tight because the roots are growing into the moss. You can even peek by unwrapping the foil, but be sure to wrap it back tightly without disturbing the tender roots that are forming.

When to Cut Off and Plant

Most people leave the air layer in place for about 6-8 months before removing it. This gives the plant time to form a healthy, fibrous root ball inside the foil enclosure. We once had an air layer that had been forgotten for two years because it was not marked with survey tape! Needless to say, it had a great root ball. Cut off the branch 4-6 inches below the root ball. This will help stabilize the branch when it is potted. Place the branch in a bucket of water for 2 to 3 hours so the roots will be well hydrated and any insects in the root ball will be eliminated.

Carefully remove the foil (or other enclosure) and plant the branch in a 1-gallon container. A larger container is not recommended because it allows the soil to stay too wet.

Plant the root ball in a pot and gently firm up the soil around the root ball taking care not to pack it too hard and damage the new roots. It may help to stake the plant to give it added stability. Be sure to label your plant!

Because the air layer was formerly supported by a large plant and now is on its own roots, it is wise to trim the branch and reduce the number of leaves. The new roots cannot support as much foliage as the mother plant did. So a good trim is the best thing you can do for a new air layer.

As with any new camellia plant, it should be gradually introduced to sunlight. At first place it in a shady area out of direct sun or wind. Keep the plant watered but not soggy or you will risk the plant developing root rot. A periodic light misting can also help the new air layer adjust to growing on its own. A new air layer should be left in the original pot until new growth appears. At that point you can introduce it to more sun, but keep it watered. Once it has rooted out into the pot, you will be able to plant the air layer in your garden or give it away and share with other camellia growers.

Many clubs have air layer "parties" where they make up to 100 air layers at a time. The goal of these events is to make new plants, which are sold as moneymakers for their club at the annual camellia show. You may even be able to "put in an order" for a special variety you want to add to your garden. It's even more fun to participate with the club and learn from others.

Rooting Cuttings

Sharing plants is a favorite pastime for camellia growers. Each year, sharing cuttings (or scion swaps) for grafting occurs in every club. From May to August, cuttings are exchanged for rooting. By that time of the year, nearly everyone has been to a show during the year and developed a "wish list" of favorites they want to acquire. If no one in your area has a variety you want, there are many places that offer scions for sale by mail order, as well.

Rooting cuttings is easy and requires only a few materials. A good container and rooting medium and is about all you need. The beauty of rooting cuttings is that in almost all cases you will get an exact duplicate of the plant you want.

Some camellias are genetically unstable and have mutations or "sports" of the original bloom. (These have produced some fantastic new blooms!). If you get cuttings from one of those branches, the bloom will be a variation of the original – known as a "sport." But some sports have been known to rival the original bloom and are very desirable. Gardeners who discover a nice sport will often tag the branch so they can go back and take cuttings.

The best way to root cuttings is to "stick" them right away after they have been cut. If this is not possible, you can store them up to a couple weeks in a refrigerator. The fresher the cutting, the more successful you will be, and it helps to have everything prepared ahead of time so you can stick them immediately.

Rooting Materials
• Sharp clippers
• Rubbing alcohol
• Sand or Perlite
• Peat moss
• Container for rooting
• Rooting hormone (powder or liquid)
• Rooting Media

There are many opinions about which rooting medium is

the best but a general consensus is to use equal parts of (1) Perlite or sand and (2) peat moss. Courser grades of sand or Perlite are better because they do not compact as much. The new roots of a cutting grow best in a light airy medium, which prevents the tender new roots from dampening off (rotting). The medium therefore should drain well and not suffocate the new roots.

To get new cuttings off to a good start, the rooting medium should be sanitary, free of contamination. Scooping up sand from the garden or recycling old peat moss may introduce fungus, weeds, and insects to the environment you are trying to create. Pre-packaged media is ideal.

Rooting Containers

The main feature to look for in a container is good drainage. Choose a container with holes large enough to let water easily drain through. Some gardeners reuse old plastic pots, which is fine if you wash it with a weak solution of bleach and let it dry before adding the medium. A popular container for rooting is the cell pack that holds 25-50 cuttings, each in its own section. These save both space and medium.

Collecting Cuttings

This is the fun part! You may have waited all year for cuttings of a special plant. Your containers are ready, and now is the time to visit friends to gather cuttings. Look for healthy cuttings that have hardened off from the latest year's growth (meaning they are not still green). Cut them back a few inches to the joint where the current year's growth began, taking a cutting with about five nodes. The new roots will grow from the nodes once they are stuck in the rooting medium.

Ideally cuttings should be taken early in the day when

the plant is not dry or stressed. There is always some degree of failure with any propagation technique, even for experienced gardeners. So do take a few cuttings from each plant but don't overcut your welcome! If you happen to find, as we have, and old abandoned garden or nursery, then cut all you want.

As with grafting and air layering, rooting requires a little bit of plant surgery. Clean, sharp tools are essential. A bottle or rubbing alcohol is useful to sterilize your clippers.

Place cuttings in a plastic bag with a slightly damp paper towel and keep them out of direct sunlight. Some gardeners like to keep them in a dark bag or bucket with a lid. Remember, you can store them in the fridge for a couple weeks but they do better when stuck in rooting medium right away, so don't delay.

Sticking the Cuttings

Carefully remove all but two leaves from the stem. Instead of pulling them off which can rip out the growth nodes, cut the leaves off as close to each node as you can. Roots will form at the nodes. Cut the remaining top two leaves in half to reduce the transpiration. Like trimming a stem for grafting, shave off a small section of bark from one side of the lower end of each cutting. This will encourage callusing and root formation along the exposed surface.

Dip the end of each stem in rooting hormone. If using liquid, allow it to dry before inserting the stem into the medium. Most liquid hormone solutions are alcohol-based so they dry quickly. If using hormone powder wet the stem first, dip it in hormone powder, then shake off the excess.

Poke a small hole in the medium with a pencil or nail so the powder is not brushed off as you insert the cutting into the medium. Then gently firm up the medium around the cutting. If containers are large enough to root several cuttings, make sure the cuttings are at least 2 inches apart so they will have ample room for root development.

Caring for the Cuttings

The most critical part of rooting cuttings is caring for them while they develop roots. The leaves need a humid environment to stay alive without any roots. But if the medium is too wet the cuttings will rot; too dry and they will wither. Either way, your effort is wasted. But with a little care and attention they will thrive and grow roots in 6-7 weeks.

The best environment is damp and warm. Consistency is important here. Some growers have elaborate systems that include bottom heating, or they create plastic tents to pro-duce a microclimate. In all cases, be sure to keep your cuttings out of direct sun, which stress the cuttings.

Tenting the cuttings does have some advantages: constant humidity and protection from squirrels. Cuttings in cell trays with multiple sections can be covered with plastic supported by wire or sticks to create a mini greenhouse. A soda bottle with the bottom removed also works well as a cover. The cap can be removed and adjusted to control the humidity.

Has it Rooted Yet?

Some camellias root more easily than others. Most japonicas and sasanquas will root in 6-7 weeks. Camellia reticulata is notoriously difficult to root and is best propagated by grafting. To find out if a cutting has rooted, tug slightly on the stem. If you feel some resistance, then roots are developing. It is best to leave cuttings in their container until mid to late winter, which is about 5-6 months depending on when they were planted. Once they develop good roots you can dispense with the tents and plastic covers but still treat them with care.

Hardening Off

As with any tender new plant, a cutting needs to harden off before being removed and replanted into a larger pot. Avoid extremes of wind and sun during this process. When exposing it to sun, be sure it is morning sun and partially shaded for the first few months. When transplanting into a one-gallon pot, regular planting mix is fine. Be careful not to crush the new roots when tamping the soil. The newly rooted plants can stay in a one-gallon pot for a year or longer until it develops a good root system.

Planting Seeds

Growing plants from seed is challenging but rewarding. Camellias do not bloom "true" from seed, which means a seedling is never identical to the parent. It is also rare to produce a unique new flower from a seedling, but if you do get a beauty, you have something very special. And you can name it as a new variety!

Even though other methods of propagation such as grafting or air layering are faster and produce larger plants more quickly, the thrill of possibly discovering a worthwhile new seedling is what keeps many camellia growers and hybridizers planting seeds each year. And even if you never produce a unique new bloom, you will have free plants to use for rootstock so nothing is wasted.

A quick caveat may be in order regarding the amount of time it takes for a new seedling to bloom. Under normal circumstances, a seedling requires 5-10 years before it produces its first bloom. This requires great patience, which is why growing camellias from seed is generally less popular among average camellia growers as a source of new garden plants. Nevertheless there is much satisfaction in growing camellias from seed, as an easy, educational and inexpensive way to get produce new plants. And you never know when you may end up with a real keeper!

Materials	
• Fungicide	• Ziploc bags
• Potting soil	• Sphagnum moss

Racing the Squirrels

Camellia seeds mature in late summer and early fall. They grow inside seedpods, which appear like small fruit growing on a camellia plant. When the seedpod ripens, it begins to dry and crack open, releasing the seeds, which fall to the ground. You can beat the squirrels to them, however,  by picking the seed pods just as they are beginning to ripen. It is better to pick them when you see them rather than wait until later when they may be gone. Set any unopened seed pods aside until they dry and open. Remove the seeds for planting.

Getting Off to a Good Start

Camellia seeds are very hard, so soaking them in water

overnight will aid in germination. Spray the seeds lightly with fungicide after they have been soaked. The seeds can be easily germinated in a plastic bag filled with sphagnum moss. Moisten the moss, add the seeds and seal the bag, which should be kept in a warm place away from direct sun. As seeds germinate, a taproot emerges, and you can remove the seed from the plastic bag to be planted in a small pot. Treat it carefully, however, so as not to injure the new root.

Planting and Transplanting

Un-germinated seeds can also be placed in a pot atop a good layer of soil and pressed lightly into the soil. Then cover it with another thin layer of additional soil and water in the seeds. This method lends itself to the planting of many seeds in a single pot, resulting in many seedlings, which can be separated for potting later.

Once a seedling produces several leaves, it can be transplanted into one-gallon or smaller container. Cutting off the tip end of the taproot will induce a more fibrous root system, which is helpful if planting in a pot. It is best to leave a young seedling in a pot for a year or longer. This ensures good root formation and gradual hardening off of the new plant before it is placed in the garden.

It is also possible to plant seeds directly in the ground, where the taproot can be left intact. A wire screen above the planting area may be used to protect the seed from squirrels. A seedling grown directly in the growth will have the opportunity to extend its taproot, making the plant stronger and more drought resistant once it grows into a mature plant.

If you have kept track of the seed parent, you may want to make a label with the name of the parent in the event your seedling later produces a fantastic bloom that you decide to keep and name. It will be interesting and helpful to have a record of the seed parentage for future reference.

Hybridizing

Camellia growers who want to try their hand at crossing varieties and species to produce new plants are the dedicated few that give Mother Nature a helping hand by pollinating plants artificially. It is these hybridizers to whom we average gardeners owe a debt of gratitude for the many new varieties and hybrids now entering the market.

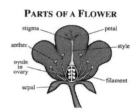

PARTS OF A FLOWER

Rather than entrusting the pollination process to bees and other random sources, hybridizers carefully select certain plants to hand pollinate in order to produce a higher percentage of quality blooms – all in the hope of producing a unique new variety that possesses the best qualities of the parent plants and is desirable to gardeners.

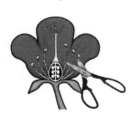

The process of hand pollination is relatively complex and involves isolating the intended mother bloom before it opens, and cutting away all unopened flower petals until an ovary develops. The stamen of the emasculated bud is then sprinkled with pollen from the father plant. The hand-pollinated bud is then covered with a paper bag to prevent other pollen from reaching the ovary until fertilization is complete in about 10-14 days.

The goal of this process is to produce a seed pod from the hand-pollinated bud, which produces seed that can be germinated, planted and later inspected when it blooms. This is a very painstaking process requiring years of planning, recordkeeping and care. The entire process can take several years from start to finish as a new seedling is nurtured toward producing its first bloom.

Hybridizing, however, can be very rewarding for the dedicated grower or hobbyist who seeks to develop something new. Further instruction can be found on the ACS website or in most camellia books.

 # Grafting Reminders

Always choose healthy rootstock and scions. Previous hard freezes may have damaged the cambium layers of either or both. Examine scions for evidence of brown or dead tissue.

Make sure the cambium layers of the rootstock and scion are align correctly and make a clear contact point.

Be careful not to knock the scion out of alignment when covering or uncovering the graft.

Maintain high humidity under the covering of the graft. Check the sealing sand around the bottom of the covering. Keep the soil lightly moist. Soil too wet encourages fungal infection.

The covering of the graft must be shaded.

Do not remove the covering container too quickly, replace it if tender growth starts to wilt.

Be careful not to let shoots coming from the stock below the graft choke out the desired growth from the scion. The scion shoots should not grow too vigorously because they break more easily.

 # Hybrid Camellias

The first modern hybrid camellias were produced in Britain during the 1930s by John Charles Williams. Whether the result of intentional cross-pollination or a lucky accident of japonica pollen naturally deposited on a sasanquas is a matter of debate. Nonetheless, C. williamsii, named for its grower, became the first modern hybrid to be recognized officially as a new species. Initially, williamsii hybrids were limited to pink blooms of varying soft shades. Later, however, other hybridizers developed cultivars like 'Anticipation' that produced blooms of deep red. Williamsii varieties remain the largest group of hybrids, but current research continues and the possibilities appear endless.

Troubleshooting Camellias

Reading the Tea Leaves

Camellias are very hardy and have few natural enemies. The same healthful qualities in tea are perhaps a clue to their above average resistance to disease and insects. When problems arise, however, the message is often in its leaves!

Without a doubt, the greatest threat to a camellia is the harm we do ourselves by planting too low, over-fertilizing, or letting a plant dry out. Assuming the problem is not self-inflicted, the issue may be insects, disease, soil minerals, or climate.

Such problems are relatively rare, but it helps to know how to recognize them immediately. The key to preventing major damage is frequent observation (a regular garden walk) coupled with early diagnosis and treatment.

Systemic Problems

A camellia plant is a like a machine. To diagnose and fix a breakdown you need a basic knowledge of how the machine works. A struggling camellia will generally signal through its leaves what needs fixing. The working parts of this botanical machine are its roots (fuel supply), trunk (plumbing), and foliage (reactor).

When working properly, a camellia's roots absorb water, nitrogen, and minerals from the soil. They are then pumped upward to the foliage above ground. The trunk and limbs serve as its plumbing. Unlike water pipes, the trunk and limbs carry sap along an outer ring, just beneath the bark, freeing the inner heartwood to provide structural support. The larger a plant's foliage, the better root system and plumbing it needs.

A camellia's foliage, when functioning properly, absorbs sunlight as well as nitrogen, carbon dioxide, and other gases from the air. The working part of a leaf is on both sides, as even the underside contains important pores (known as stomata) that open and close, absorbing gases and moisture from the atmosphere.

These three main parts, working together, enable a reaction called photosynthesis to occur. This combines the various fuel elements with the sun's energy to create a continually expanding (i.e. growing) organism whose cells are arranged by DNA into a certain plant – the camellia! A camellia is extremely high in carbon (stored energy) as evidenced by its fuel-grade seed oil and its extremely dense wood. The heartwood of a camellia is truly among the hardest and heaviest on earth.

If a breakdown occurs in any of the camellia's three main parts – roots, trunk, or leaves – it stops working. Its leaves will telegraph a distress signal indicating the problem. But even S-O-S means nothing without understanding code.

Here, then, are some code lessons for reading camellia leaves, followed by a more detailed discussion of specific diseases, pests and other issues that you may encounter.

Root Problems

If a camellia's leaves start wilting or become discolored, it generally means trouble underground. The roots may have gotten dry and stopped supplying water to the leaves, which then wilt and (if not immediately remedied) fall off. In severe instances, the plant is mortally weakened. However, those exact same symptoms – wilting leaves -- can also indicate that the roots have *too much* water and are totally waterlogged. If roots remain saturated in water for an extended time, they suffocate from lack of air. A root fungus, which often is fatal, may also produce the same symptoms of overall leaf wilt. For the above reasons, when a camellia's leaves wilt all over, the starting point is to check the soil moisture before diagnosing the problem.

Stunted growth and/or leaf discoloration is another symptom of a problem in the root zone. Camellia roots malfunction if they are poisoned (as by a toxic chemical) or if the soil pH and minerals are not suitably balanced for its roots to absorb enough nitrogen and iron to stay healthy and green. Different species and varieties (including their hybrids) may sometimes exhibit different soil preferences.

Consider for example the occasional healthy looking plant in no apparent distress but which hardly grows! The green leaves indicate all systems are working, but their subtle message is that the plant is sinking below ground level, or that a slight imbalance exists in the soil minerals or pH limiting the roots' ability to absorb nutrients for growth. After checking to ensure that the plant has not sunk below the normal ground level, a short-term solution may be a foliar fertilizer spray, while the longer solution is a soil test to determine what fertilizer may correct the imbalance.

Even a healthy camellia can turn sick if its roots outgrow

the amended soil and come into contact with something very bad, like remnants of crumbly concrete left in the soil. Camellias thrive in acidic soils (a pH range of 5-6) and concrete contains lime, which is alkaline and toxic. Once again, the leaves will signal a problem in the root zone.

Finally, wilted leaves can also appear when a plant suffers root loss from being dug and transplanted. If that occurs, the foliage can be pruned to balance with the roots. Otherwise it may decline because the roots cannot supply enough moisture to serve the outsized foliage.

Trunk Problems

A camellia's leaves may also indicate a problem with the trunk, which is its plumbing. Assuming normal water and soil conditions, the leaves will show immediate distress if the main trunk is severely wounded, as with a weed trimmer or a chewing animal.

When only a portion of the foliage shows distress, it means a limb is physically wounded or broken, disrupting the sap flow. If an inspection reveals no physical wound, those distressed leaves (confined to only a portion of the plant) almost certainly indicate the presence of a disease that is infecting the branch or trunk, killing some of the bark tissue and thereby disrupting the sap at a point below the dying foliage. The source of the disease must be immediately located and treated if possible (generally by removal of all affected tissue) before it spreads like cancer to the entire plant.

In large plants, trunk damage can also occur from causes like woodpeckers that damage the outer (cambium) layer of bark and interfere with the sap flow, producing anemic looking foliage. Although it is not strictly necessary to remove the damaged portion, the remainder of the plant will benefit.

Leaf Problems

Sometimes the leaves themselves may stop working properly, disrupting the plant's photosynthetic food-production. However, seldom are all the leaves damaged at once. An exception is where the plant suffers an extreme freeze, from which it may rebound if the trunk is not killed to the ground. Fire has the same effect. In these cases, there is no question about the cause.

Occasionally, however, a camellia's leaves may become severely damaged by a sudden insect infestation, such as spider mites. A bronzing and graying of the leaves is a telltale sign of spider mites. It is astonishing how quickly these tiny creatures (barely visible) can overtake and suck the juice from healthy camellia leaves, leaving the plant weakened and discolored. This can happen almost overnight if not caught and treated in time.

More often than not, leaf damage to a camellia is confined to less than the entire plant and results from only minor insect damage or climate conditions. The most common cause is sucking insects, particularly tea scale, evidenced by a white cottony coating on the underside of an infested leaf.

Excess fertilization can cause leaf damage, which appears in the form of brown tips. Leaf damage can also occur from algae scabs that are relatively harmless. Climatic damage occurs in the form of freeze burn or sunscald.

Camellia Insect Control

When camellias feel the wake-up call of spring so do insects. Spiders, aphids, and mites – oh my! Leaf-chewing beetles emerge from winter slumber with big appetites that may leave a camellia's foliage looking like Swiss cheese. Thirsty spider mites can suck a camellia's leaves dry. Scale insects burrow into the underbelly of its fleshy leaves, turning them mottled yellow.

The good news is, nearly all these pests can be controlled with a single product – a horticultural spray containing a waxy "summer oil" ingredient that is sold under trade names like *Ultra-Fine* or *Sun Spray* at garden centers. This spray essentially smothers the insects and is applied with either a hose-end or pump sprayer. Unlike "dormant oil" (recommended for professionals) these products can be applied year round.

A spray treatment in early spring and fall is helpful for prevention and you should certainly spray when infestation appears. It is very important that the spray be applied copiously to the underside of leaves where bugs hide. This can be a messy job around large camellias (you will get wet) but spraying the top surface alone is ineffective. And these sprays are harmless to humans.

For severe infestations, it may be necessary to add some insecticide to the spray mix, such as *Malathion*, but that is suggested only as a last resort since you have to be more careful. It is better to be safe and environmentally friendly. Your body will appreciate it, too.

Tea Scale

Yellow-mottled leaves with a white cottony underside are a sure sign of tea scale (often called camellia scale). The leaf mottling results from the loss of chlorophyll that is sucked out by the insects from the underside. An examination of the leaf's underside reveals a white cotton-like substance that serves as a protective tent for the tiny black-scaled insects that attach themselves to the underside surface. The good news is, scale is usually a sign of a healthy plant.

Scale insects generally are found on the lower branches but work their way upward if left untreated. Scale is seldom fatal but does affect a plant's appearance. The infested leaves can eventually be weakened to a point where, if not controlled, an entire branch or section of the plant will look unhealthy, leading to the loss of foliage and dead twigs.

The best treatment for scale is the aforementioned "summer oil" spray, which can be applied year round without damage. These products are often made from the plant oils of the sunflower or canola plant, and are environmentally safe. Insecticidal soaps also work. The spray is applied with a hose end sprayer or pump sprayer.

The most important thing to remember in treating tea scale is to spray the underside of the leaves thoroughly. Spraying only the top surface is ineffective. Serious infestations may require multiple applications.

Spider Mites

A sudden bronze to gray discoloration of leaves is pretty strong evidence of spider mites. The discoloration appears in its earliest stages along the leaf spine (where the leaf is thickest). It then spreads to the entire leaf as the infestation worsens, causing the leaves to change color from green to bronze to ash-gray. Some may fall off.

Quick action is the key to stopping this. Spider mite damage can occur very suddenly because they reproduce quickly -- especially in hot dry weather during late summer and fall. These are very small pests (barely visible) that suck juices from the underside of leaves. When populations are high, they produce fine webs resembling spider webs.

If damage already has occurred, take heart. The plant

119

may look terrible for a season, but it sprouts new foliage the following year. Take it also as a warning to keep a close eye on that same plant in the future because spider mites seem drawn repeatedly to certain plants and locations.

The most common treatment for light infestations is the same "summer oil" used for tea scale. Insecticidal soap or *Neem* oil may also be effective. Major infestations can require multiple applications, including the use of chemical miticides or insecticides to gain the upper hand. By experimenting with different products, you will find what works best for you.

Once again, *quick timing* is the most important factor – more so than waiting to shop for a good product. A household mixture of soap and water may work in the short-term to stem an outbreak, affording time to locate other products if needed to treat a severe infestation.

Aphids (plant lice)

Tiny flea-sized insects gathering on new leaf shoots are probably aphids. There is no need to panic, as they cause only minor harm. If not controlled, aphids can leave some of the new leaves curled, crinkled or distorted. Aphids do have many natural enemies such as ladybugs and certain wasps, so chemical control is often unnecessary. Some growers even order supplies of "good bugs" such as ladybugs (available from Internet retailers) that are released into the garden to control aphids and other insects. When treatment is necessary, an insecticidal soap is usually adequate, and even a strong blast of water from a garden hose can wash them away. The same "summer oil" used on scale and spider mites also works well.

White Flies

Sooty black mold on camellia leaves, or a flurry of white

winged insects when foliage is rustled, means you probably have white flies. These insects appear in early to mid-summer and feed on the sugar in the leaves, leaving behind a sticky honeydew. The honeydew, once it molds, gives the leaf surface a soot-covered appearance. The harm is mostly cosmetic although in severe cases this sooty mold can stunt a plant's growth by interfering with the leaves' ability to absorb sunlight. Insecticidal soap usually rinses away the mold and chases away the white flies.

Leaf Eating Beetles

Holes chewed in leaves are generally a sign of beetles. These culprits are rarely more than a nuisance to camellia gardeners, and their control is often more trouble than it is worth. Most beetles feed at night and are few in number, so you often can spot them by flashlight and pick them off. (Suggestion: warn your neighbors before prowling around in the bushes with a flashlight!) Since beetles generally crawl up the trunk, a control method is to wrap a sticky band around the trunk, which creates a barrier. Another use for duct tape! The band should be at least two inches wide and sticky enough to retain its tackiness for an extended period. Commercial banding products are also available.

Camellia Disease Control

Camellias are rugged and very disease resistant, especially well-established camellias. However, there are a few natural fungal diseases that may be native in your garden but are not very friendly to our oriental plant guests. In fact, they can be quite rude. Here are some diseases to watch out for.

Dieback Disease

If the foliage wilts or dies on only a *part* of a camellia plant, the cause is often a fungal disease known as "die back."

Its formal name is *Glomerella cingulata*, a fungus that enters the bark of a camellia and begins to spread like cancer, progressively eating away the woody tissue it touches and leaving an open wound that often is referred to as a "canker."

Upon discovering a branch that is dead or dying, through no apparent physical injury, inspect it closely. Trace downward along the affected branch and trunk until you find the source of infection. If not treated immediately, the fungus can spread throughout the plant. In a young or small plant it often is fatal. If no canker is found, remove the affected branch entirely and monitor closely for further symptoms.

If a canker or lesion is found, the only treatment is to immediately remove all infected wood. At a minimum the bad limb or branch should be cut away well below the point of infection until you reach wood that is disease-free, "green and clean" as we say. If you see any discoloration, such as black spot in the heartwood, keep cutting it back until the wood is clear. Ideally treat the remaining cut surface with a fungicide such as *Captan* or *Benlate*.

If the disease is found along a main trunk, especially low near the ground, the problem is very grave. At a minimum this requires some major surgery, removing all infected wood. Perhaps the infection can be carved away until the wood is clear of disease, but this is difficult and may leave a gaping wound that should be treated with a fungicidal patch for a time. For most gardeners, it often is easier and safer to cut the entire plant back to below the canker (until you reach healthy green wood) and let it re-grow, or remove the plant entirely. If that seems drastic, you can try removing as much infected wood as possible and wait to see if the plant rebounds.

The important thing is to eliminate the active diseased

wood from the garden so it does not spread to other plants, and discard all infected wood in the garbage (or by burning) and not by throwing it onto a garden trash pile where the disease may spread. Keep in mind that a live *Glomerella* fungus can spread if left in the garden, which is why you dispose of all infected wood.

In hot humid regions with heavy rainfall, some gardeners practice prevention by spraying their camellias with a systemic fungicide once or twice a year. This generally is most effective at first flush during the two main growing periods, which are early spring and late summer as old leaves are being shed. However, the best prevention of all is regular inspection and immediate attention.

Root Rot

The sudden wilting of an entire plant (assuming no moisture issues) is often a sign of root rot. This more commonly affects young plants, and only rarely will it affect a mature plant with an established root system. In fact, the difference in symptoms (wilting of an entire plant versus only a branch) is one of the ways of recognizing the difference between die back and root rot. Die back is usually confined to only a portion of the plant.

Root rot occurs from a soil-borne fungus *(Phytophthora cinnamomi)* that occurs in poorly drained soils or in low spots that drain poorly in periods of sustained heavy rain. If the roots can be inspected either in the ground or by lifting the plant, they reveal dark discoloration, ranging from orange (early stages) to black (totally dead). Normal camellia roots are gray or white.

The fungus can travel by underground water migration and often stays active in the soil. If caught early enough, the only treatment is a soil drench of fungicide such as *Subdue* or similar. Unfortunately, however, the disease is nearly always fatal in a young plant, requiring its removal and disposal -- ideally including the soil in the immediate root zone.

In regions where root rot is prevalent, the most common prevention is to grow varieties that are resistant. While the species *C. japonica* is more susceptible to root rot, other species like *C. sasanqua* are not. Varieties such as 'Kanjiro' and 'Daydream' are highly resistant and vigorous growers. They therefore are often selected as a rootstock for *C. japonica* grafts.

Japonicas grafted onto the "borrowed" roots of these varieties generally grow very well, even in climates where root rot is otherwise a threat to japonicas grown on their own roots. For this reason, many camellia gardeners in high-risk areas often choose to plant only grafted camellias using understock from a sasanqua or other resistant species.

Twig Blight

This term describes what happens when a fungus similar to die back attacks the twigs of a camellia. It may not completely destroy a plant but kills smaller limbs and twigs. In a large camellia the presence of twig blight can damage the entire canopy, leaving behind dead and leafless stems in a canopy that looks sick all over. Such plants are often stunted and produce fewer and weaker blooms.

The injury is produced by a fungus named *Colletotrichum gloesporioides* that first enters through a fresh wound or leaf scar. It then travels horizontally, constricting the flow of nutrients to the foliage and stems above the infection. Next the disease travels vertically up and down a stem, causing the entire stem or twig to die. It can spread to leaf wounds on other stems through splashes of water during a rain. Soon a mature camellia canopy is affected all over by twig blight.

The only treatment for twig blight is to prune out all dead or diseased stems back to healthy wood. In cases of severe twig blight in a mature plant, the best practice is often a major pruning of the entire canopy to rehabilitate the plant, which generally returns to its original vigor.

Petal Blight

Camellia blooms that turn prematurely brown or exhibit brown freckles are usually symptomatic of a fungal disease called "petal blight" or "flower blight." There currently is no known cure, and many camellia organizations have set up a substantial cash reward for anyone who finds a cure.

The fungus that causes petal blight (*Ciborinia camelliae*) grows in the soil or mulch beneath camellia plants where old blooms have fallen and decayed. It becomes active in humid climates during cycles of cold and warm temperatures. The damage results from fungal spores that infect a flower's petals, or sometimes (in severe cases) enter the moist interior of a bloom turning it brown from the inside. These spores can travel hundreds of yards by wind, infecting blooms on nearby plants as well.

The only prevention is good sanitation, ridding the garden of fungus by removing all spent blooms annually. This is highly impractical, however, especially in a large garden. Moreover, if you live in a neighborhood of camellias, it is virtually impossible to eliminate all petal blight. One method of limiting the disease is to replace all mulch annually. Some growers also have tried various fungicides, with only limited success.

Petal blight has become a fact of life in most parts of the camellia belt, where growers have learned to cope and enjoy them regardless. When cutting blooms for indoors, the best time is in the morning, immediately after they open and before heavy exposure to blight-ridden air. You can also try cutting flowers when the blight is noticeably less active. Keeping blooms in a cool dry environment slows the affect. There also are some varieties that are more resistant to the affect of petal blight, so ask local gardeners what works best.

Other Diseases and Disorders
Leaf Gall

An unsightly growth of thick fleshy distorted leaves on the end of a branch (usually on *C. sasanqua*) is known as leaf gall. These are generally harmless and eventually turn dry and fall off. If bothersome, they can be removed by hand and thrown away. Removal also reduces the future occurrence of gall.

Lichens

A lichen is a flaky gray combination of algae and fungus that occasionally appears on a camellia trunk or stem. Lichens are not parasitic and usually do not harm the plant. However, since they cannot attach to a stem that is aspirating normally, their appearance is a signal the plant is not growing vigorously. The best control is to improve the plant's maintenance.

Sunscald

Leaves that appear burned are often a result of too much sun, especially on newly planted camellias that have not adjusted to their new location in a garden. This can also result from a "rainy" sunshine (when water drops magnify the sun's rays) or frost-covered leaves that receive early sun. If the problem persists over time, the only solution is to move a plant to a different spot.

Weed poison

A flush of small severely deformed leaves on a camellia

is often a symptom of overspray from a glyphosate-based weed killer like *Roundup*. The symptoms are most severe with *Roundup Pro* to which camellias are highly allergic at the slightest whiff. If an overspray was minor a plant may outgrow the toxicity, but severe exposure is often fatal. Sad to say, the plant's death is slow and gruesome to watch. The message is clear – use herbicides carefully around camellias, and never on a windy day.

A final note on chemicals: Although camellia diseases, insects, and weeds may leave gardeners with little choice but to use chemical controls, there is no substitute for conscientious care and maintenance. Camellias have an advantage over many ornamentals in their ability to withstand most natural threats. Still, if chemical controls are necessary, the label directions on any garden chemical must be followed.

 ## Set Them Free

If there is any downside to creating your own private camellia collection, it is later realizing the fact of their (or rather your) impermanence. Every veteran grower knows of a once-great camellia garden that fell victim to "progress" after the owners were gone.

It is no exaggeration that our personal affection for camellias has caused them to be grown in virtual captivity. There is no question this accounts for why camellias are not in greater demand by today's average gardener. The vast majority of the gardening public has never seen anything like the majestic camellias hidden away in our personal gardens. But anything so storied and beautiful deserves to be enjoyed by everyone. It is time to set them free!

Fortunately a perfect opportunity exists right around the corner: our public gardens and landscapes. Camellias are long-lived (hundreds of years) and unsurpassed in their ease of maintenance, making them ideal for public spaces. Public gardens, colleges, churches, cemeteries, and government buildings are all places where camellias can be left alone and enjoyed for their natural beauty -- perhaps for centuries.

It was not very long ago that camellias did have a place of honor in public landscapes. Examples are the handsome Capitol grounds in Sacramento, the beautiful Bonaventure Cemetery in Savannah, and the stately Spring Hill College campus in Mobile – camellia treasuries gifted decades ago by wise and generous gardeners as a lasting legacy.

As you learn more about camellias, make it a priority to find ways to share them with the public. Volunteer at a local public garden and/or seek every opportunity to add camellias to public spaces.

Identifying Old Camellias

Everyone has wondered about the name of an old camellia variety. For many of us, that is how we contracted the camellia "bug" in the first place.

Depending on a camellia's age, it often is possible to identify it with some detective work. First look for an old metal label tied to a lower limb near the trunk. At one time, the owner knew its name and may have labeled it. Labels sometimes fall off and are found by searching the ground below. Another resource is a plant list or map kept by the owner. These often are among garden books and papers passed down with the property.

Assuming no labels or lists are found, the detective work is more challenging. Ask an experienced grower to visit your garden in bloom to identify your plants, which often is possible, especially among the more famous varieties. Another option is to carry blooms to a camellia show and ask for help. Public gardens are another great source of guidance.

Yet another approach is to take a close-up photo and email it to an experienced grower or to one of the many camellia organizations, asking for identification.

There also are books with hundreds of photos of named blooms and websites with "photo galleries" of camellia varieties arranged in a helpful index. In hard cases, such as a very old garden, one can sometimes research vintage nursery catalogues from when the camellias likely were planted.

Finally, bear in mind that many old gardens have camellias that are unique seedlings never registered by the owner. In that event you can satisfy yourself with having inherited a one-of-a-kind treasure!

Did You Know?

- Petal blight was first discovered in Japan in 1919. As early as 1938, the fungus showed up in plants in California, and within 20 years it had spread throughout the "Camellia Belt" of the United States.
- Blooms infected with the petal blight virus fall to the ground and eventually produce a sclerotium in the base of the bloom; these sclerotia provide protection and food for the fungus. The fungus survive within these structures until the following year or even longer–sclerotia may lie dormant in the soil up to 4 years.

Saving Old Camellias
Senior Citizens of Distinction

Some of the most impressive camellias are the very old ones that have undergone a makeover. Whether one plant or many, a new owner of an old plant has several options short of removal, all of which yield excellent results. And because large camellias take a lifetime to grow, they are truly priceless and irreplaceable – well worth saving.

An overgrown or worn out camellia, having declined in quality through neglect or old age, is dramatically rejuvenated by heavy pruning. It may resemble a plucked chicken for a time, but within a couple of years it will be stunning in its handsomeness, thick in foliage, and loaded with outstanding blooms.

A story is told of Mr. A. A. Hunt, curator of Bellingrath Gardens in the mid-twentieth century, whom a visitor once asked, "What are the really rare and scarce ones?" Without hesitation he replied, "The old ones." Imagine one who inherits an attic of Monets and Rembrandts, only to unknowingly toss them on the trash pile!

A large camellia won't equal the value of a Monet but it appraises very highly, precisely because of its age and size. Such a plant generally is unavailable for purchase, so owning one is the special privilege of only a few. And on rare occasions when a large camellia must be removed, one often can have it dug and transplanted by local nurseryperson or landscaper who will dig and re-sell it (at a handsome price) to someone planning a high-end landscape.

Restoring Old Plants

To rejuvenate an old camellia, prune it back to its basic architectural skeleton, 2-3 feet above ground, shaping the remaining limbs to suit taste and location. Camellias can even  be cut back to a 12-inch stump when necessary, and they will grow back with renewed vigor. If you find that too shocking, then prune it back as far as you are comfortable. The trunk and limbs of a camellia have hidden growth buds that sprout and begin growing in only a few months.

There is a saying about camellias, "spare the shears and spoil the plant." Some varieties will re-grow more quickly than others, depending on their variety, growth habit, and the amount of sun they receive.

Gardeners new to such hard pruning may be hesitant at first. Cutting the limbs of an old camellia back to leafless stubs takes courage. But when the new growth returns with a vigor that was lost in the old plant, they will find their courage well rewarded!

Just remember, camellias can take it. A long established camellia is nearly indestructible. And it will impress you by how well it rebounds.

The best time for heavy pruning is during the blooming season (when the camellia is dormant) or just before the first cycle of growth in spring before the sap rises. Start by removing all weak limbs and twigs from the plant's interior. Then cut the exterior limbs back to strong healthy wood. Cut all limbs at an angle to shed water.

You will need heavy lopping shears, hand-clippers, a tree saw, and maybe even a chain saw. Keep in mind that sharpness counts -- the sharper a tool, the more quickly the plant will heal. Plus it makes the work much easier on the hands and shoulders!

Depending on the height of a camellia, an attractive alternative to cutting it back is to limb it up into tree form. The results may be very surprising. It produces the same rejuvenating affect for the plant, which will be fuller and healthier at the top. Many people are unaware that camellias are small understory trees in their native habitat, so they look very natural when pruned in this manner.

Bear in mind, however, that pruning a camellia into a tree form will put most of the blooms out of reach. So in making the decision, consider whether it is a good cut flower variety. Also, if you decide to limb it up into tree form, and if the results prove unsatisfactory, the plant can always be pruned back to a short stump and allowed to regenerate.

Another option is to graft an entirely different variety onto the large stump and watch it sprout like a beanstalk into a shrub of the new variety. However, grafting the big ones does require a bit more skill so contact a more experienced camellia grower for assistance the first time. They will be glad to assist you and often can locate a special variety suitable for grafting onto the large understock.

Restoring Old Gardens

Many times, new owners of old homes inherit a treasure of camellias on their property. These may once have been the prized collection of a previous owner or planted throughout the property in a classic garden design. While once carefully groomed and maintained, they now may be overgrown -- blocking windows or obstructing a house or garage.

At first glance, there is nothing treasure-like in the appearance of this scene. The new owner's first impulse is to "clean up" the property and improve its appearance, removing all of the seemingly worn-out plants and shrubs. This would be a mistake in regard to the camellias, but it happens and is understandable.

A similar occurrence is the large tract bought for re-development, giving way to bulldozers that clear the property before anyone realizes what was lost. Municipal ordinances often protect larger trees but those century-old camellias are quickly dispatched. A recent example is a once renowned local camellia nursery where acres of 70 year-old camellias were left behind (worth perhaps $1,000 each) until it was cleared and grubbed for a new shopping center. That barren parking lot was sparsely re-landscaped with cheap, non-blooming foliage plants. What a pity.

In all of these situations, the old camellias could have been saved with excellent results, enhancing the value and appearance of the property. A goal of many local camellia clubs is to raise awareness among realtors and developers about the value of large camellias when property changes hands.

If you should happen to acquire or inherit a property with old camellias, there are several things you can do. The first step is to attempt to identify the camellia varieties that remain. Knowing the varieties will contribute not only to their appreciation; it enables you to make better-informed decisions about their restoration.

There are many ways to go about this.

A first option is to carefully inspect each plant for a metal name label, often tied like a soldier's dog tag to a lower branch near the trunk. In some cases, plant labels may have fallen to the garden floor and can be located by searching near the trunk. If any garden books remain on the property, they may contain a list or record of the camellia varieties.

A second option is to contact local camellia growers. They often know the history of the garden and will offer to help identify the camellias.

A third option is, before doing anything drastic, wait until the camellias are in bloom and take a sample to a camellia show or club meeting where experienced growers can often identify them.

In any event, you have many options for saving the old camellias. If they are obstructing a building, they can be heavily pruned back with great results. Thinning or removing overhead trees will introduce sunshine, to which camellias respond almost immediately. The accounts of camellia owners who have lost trees through hurricane damage suggests that tree losses are often more than offset by the renewed vigor and performance of old camellias!

Camellias planted in large groups can also be cleared of old vines and undergrowth, leaving a "camellia thicket" that makes a delightfully cool respite in summer – especially if the plants are tall. Their foliage shades the summer sun, leaving the earth cool, while in winter it yields a stunning mass of blooms!

Regardless what option is chosen for restoring an old camellia collection, you will find your patience is greatly rewarded and ultimately costs less while preserving the immeasurable value of a rare landscape feature.

Did You Know?

Eat a cup of tea? In the early Colonies, like Salem, the leaves were boiled at length, creating a bitter concoction. Then the leaves were salted and eaten with butter.

Camellia Fun Projects

Camellias provide us with a lot of entertainment. We know it is fun and therapeutic to grow them and they are beautiful when brought inside to decorate our homes. But there are many other ways to have fun with camellias. You can wax them and they last longer in this beautiful, porcelain-like condition. You can even change their colors with crayons or food coloring. Camellias, both sasanquas and japonicas can be trained to be beautiful Bonsai plants. They have been used this way for centuries in Asia. And not to leave out our younger enthusiasts, there are great ways to get children interested through camellia flower hunts or playing Bloom Bingo.

Waxing Camellia Blooms

One of the most amazingly beautiful ways to preserve camellia blooms is to dip them in paraffin wax and mineral oil. This technique is easy and fun, and the wax seals in the moisture of the bloom, leaving it shining like porcelain. Waxed camellia blooms look  fabulous anywhere, and are great gifts for friends, and especially the elderly, because waxed camellias require no care whatsoever. They do not have to be placed in water, and yet they will last for weeks if done just right. The process is surprisingly simple.

Waxing Materials

- Fresh, dry camellia blooms
- 5 pounds paraffin wax (Gulfwax or canning wax)
- 1½ pints of mineral oil (drugstore variety)
- Double boiler or electric wok with temperature control
- Large bowl of ice cold water (with ice removed)
- Candy or digital thermometer

This process mainly involves selecting a freshly opened bloom, and then making sure the wax temperature is precise. If the wax is too hot, the bloom will scorch and quickly turn brown. Experience has shown that certain varieties do better and last longer when waxed because they have thicker petals. For example a white 'Imura' bloom waxes beautifully and lasts longer because of its thick petals. The best blooms for waxing are white or pink varieties because they don't reveal the waxy film after being dipped, whereas a red bloom will show the wax in the form of a light haze.

The process for waxing camellia blooms is so simple a child can do it. But first a caution: paraffin wax is highly flammable so it should never be exposed to an open flame or high temperature.

We have found the best appliance is a cooker with a temperature gauge on it. Or you can use a double boiler. You can use a candy thermometer but the best is a small digital thermometer because you can measure the temperature much more accurately. Both of these can be purchased at many local stores. Never use a regular meat thermometer because it is not accurate enough to measure the temperature of the wax. (We know this from experience!)

First heat the wax to precisely 138° to 140° F. Temperature is the single most critical part! The wax should be deep enough to fully submerge a bloom. The mineral oil should be added while the wax is being melted. Wax alone is too thick so that is why mineral oil is added. When fully melted at 138° to 140° F (remember this is critical) the wax solution will have a clear watery consistency. Keep the thermometer attached inside the wax solution to monitor the temperature constantly.

As the wax is melting and before any blooms are dipped, prepare a large bowl of ice water by melting ice cubes in the water. Also, spread around some newspaper to catch any random drops of wax or ice water, which will make cleanup much easier.

Gripping the bloom firmly by the stem and with leaves folded back in your fingers, dip the entire bloom for only a second or two. (Don't leave it too long or the petals will scorch!) Once the bloom is lifted from the wax, give it a gentle shake to let the excess wax drip back into the pot. Tip the bloom up so the wax runs into the center of the bloom.

Immediately dip the bloom gently in ice water to fully set the wax and allow the bloom to cool down. This is an important step. Don't dunk the bloom in fast. If you do, it will cause all the petals to be pushed backwards. A gentle sideways dip will help protect the petal structure of the bloom. Leave the bloom in the ice water for at least 30 seconds. This will allow the wax to firmly set, while chilling the bloom sufficiently to prevent the petals from browning. If your petals turn brown, you can be certain the wax was too warm or the bloom wasn't sufficiently cooled down soon enough.

After removing the bloom from the ice water, set it on the newspaper to dry out. Then sit back and be amazed. Waxed camellia blooms can be displayed beautifully on a plate or dish, individually or in a grouping.

More Fun with Waxing

Who says that you have to use only clear wax? It is fun to be adventurous and experiment with different colors. All you need is regular crayons. We use a smaller pot for making colored wax because we keep our big pot going all season and wax camellias for parties, friends, and garden clubs.

A white camellia can be made into any color you want by adding a crayon to the wax; yellow and blue make a bloom particularly interesting. With these colors, you can tease your friends that you have finally found that elusive yellow or blue camellia.

And who says you have to wax just camellias? There are many flowers in your garden that wax very well. Narcissus, tulip tree blooms, and roses work well. We have had great results with Amaryllis, Christmas cactus, and gardenias, too. The only reason we have not tried Magnolias is that we don't have large enough pots! Blooms with very delicate petals (such as daylilies and azaleas) do not work well. Just experiment and see what you come up with.

 Waxing Camellia Blooms

- Use only dry camellia blooms; any water drops will interfere with the waxing application and leave droplets of water in your wax.
- Instead of plunging the bloom face down into the wax (and ice water) use sweeping motions to keep the petals from being mashed flat; this jus takes a little practice.

- After a waxed bloom begins to turn brown after several days or weeks, it can be sprayed painted gold or silver to last much longer. Or spray it pink.
- A waxed bloom, just like a fresh bloom, can be preserved longer by storing it in the refrigerator in a sealed container.
- When waxing, start with the whites, then pinks, then darker ones when you wax. The temperature can be 138° F for the lighter ones, and 140° F for the darker ones.
- You can keep adding wax and oil to your pot all season. Be careful to keep the ratios below. Be sure to remove the pieces of petal or sepals that fall into it. By the end of the season, the wax will become rancid, so throw it out. Ratios for adding amounts of wax and mineral oil as you go throughout the season.

5 lbs wax: 2.5 cups of oil   2 lbs wax: 1.0 cup of oil
4 lbs wax: 2.0 cups of oil   1 lb wax: .5 cup of oil
3 lbs wax: 1.5 cups of oil

Changing Camellia Colors

When is a white camellia yellow? Or blue or green? Easy with the help of some food coloring and a couple days. This activity was in an old ACS Yearbook and was presented as a fun activity for children but it is fun for anyone.

Small, glass votive candle holders can be used to mix up strong solutions of yellow, blue, green, and red food colors. After a few different blooms, it was found that 'White Empress' worked very well. May sure the blooms are fresh then put each one in a color and wait. It will take about two days for the color to reach its maximum saturation. You will find it interesting how the stamens and just the edges of the petals absorb the color. The longer you keep them in the color the darker the color will be.

Experiment with different white ones to see the effects. Also try blooms with different color combinations. Maybe a red and white like 'Miss Charleston Variegated' or pink and white like 'Betty Sheffield Variegated' would do well in yellow or blue? How about 'China Doll' in green? Or 'Margaret Davis' or 'Nuccio's Gem' in purple? And they said this was fun just for kids!

Bonsai Camellias

Camellias have been a favorite choice for Bonsai growers for centuries. In fact, if you ever tour the U.S. National Arboretum in Washington, D.C., be sure to see some of the world's most famous examples of camellia bonsai in the arboretum's National Bonsai and Penjing Museum. One is a 100-year-old *Camellia Higo* Bonsai that was given to the United States by the late Emperor of Japan on the occasion of the U.S. Bicentennial in 1976. It is skillfully maintained by Bonsai experts from the National Arboretum.

Camellias make excellent Bonsai because of their handsome foliage and slow rate of growth. They are very popular as Bonsai because their flowers appear in profusion as with sasanquas or some have just a few spectacular blooms like japonicas. There are three camellias most commonly used for bonsai are *C. japonica*, *C. sasanqua*, and *C. reticulata*. So if you have an ugly (if that is possible), misshapen plant give Bonsai a try. You may be very pleased with the results.

Bonsai requires skills that go far beyond the scope of this publication. When considering the idea of Bonsai camellias, you probably should look more in the direction of Bonsai growers than camellia hobbyists for instruction and training. Bonsai has become very popular and there are Bonsai clubs throughout the United States. Many helpful articles are also to be found in the publications of the American Camellia Society.

Children and Camellias

Camellia Flower Hunt Game

At camellias shows we often see quite a few children who are there with parents or grandparents. These children are usually looking rather bored and fidgety. And rightly so – there is nothing for them to do. To solve this problem and get them involved in an activity we developed a Camellia Flower Hunt Game for them.

You have seen these in a variety of settings: Children get a small book and go around and collect names, stamps, or signatures to fill up their book for a small prize. We created one where the children go around and collect names of camellias. They loved it! For prizes we had small stuffed animals, notebooks, frames – things that cost about $1 each, which was well worth the meager investment. Or you could do this in your garden with your children or grandchildren when they visit.

The game cards were pink, of course, and stapled to look like a small book. Spaces were provided where they could write the answers. You could put the name of your club on the front. The questions were:

Section 1 Ask a camellia club member .....
> Where did camellias originally come from?
> When do camellias bloom?
> What is a popular drink made from a type of camellia?

143

Section 2 Find the name of a camellia with these forms: There were photos of each form and each is identified as single, formal double, etc.

Section 3 Find the name of a camellia that is red, pink, white, red and white, pink and white.

Section 4 Find the name of a camellia that is a woman, man, a foreign name.

Section 5 Find a really small camellia, a really large camellia, your favorite camellia.

Children turned them in for a prize. This is an excellent way to get children involved with learning about camellias, gives them something to do at shows, and affords the adults time to enjoy looking at all the blooms.

Bloom Bingo Game

It is very easy to make a Bingo game of camellia blooms. All you need is photos. There are many web sites where you can download beautiful photos of blooms. You will certainly find more photos than you can ever use. The sites also give the names, which is a big help.

Create a 5 x 5 table on a regular sheet of 8 ½" x 11" paper and insert a photo into each square. Include a FREE space in the middle. You will need to make several different playing sheets so that everyone does not Bingo at the same time. At the top of the columns put BLOOM instead of BINGO. Print all of the blooms to use as the cards to call out the names. If you have access to a laminating machine this will help to extend the life of the sheets. Children (and adults) can learn the names of these beautiful blooms while having fun at the same time!

So you see, having fun with camellias and doing fun

projects is limited only by your imagination. A final "game" you can play and a caution: One of the authors agreed to pay his son $1 for each camellia the young man could identify when they were riding around town. Luckily, the son did not seem to be interested in camellias. This could have become expensive!

 ## Tie-Dyed Camellias

Many blooms have white splotches like they were tie-dyed. This is called "variegation" and is generally highly desirable. Plant developers, upon discovering a new solid color variety, often introduce a color-breaking virus to give the bloom an interesting variegation.

Two types of variegation are seen in camellias. One has clearly defined white splotches on part or nearly all of a bloom. Another is a more tie-dyed look, known as moiré (moy-RAY), in which the white coloration is streaked and blurred, which is rare and more highly valued.

There are two ways variegation occurs in camellias, one natural and another artificial. The natural variegation comes from the plant's DNA and produces a consistent color pattern. The artificial variegation occurs through a "virus" strain that is introduced either intentionally or accidentally, causing the blooms (and often some leaves) to have varying degrees of white coloration.

Serious plant collectors pay close attention to variegated strains of certain varieties, and they often seek scions for grafting from a known strain -- a pedigree of sorts – more likely to match the original plant they want to duplicate.

A number of factors affect the degree of variegation in a virus-strained camellia, such as the strength of the virus, the soil pH, soil minerals, and whether it was a grafted plant.

An accidental color-breaking virus can enter when a solid camellia is grafted onto a white rootstock or a plant's roots cross those of a white variety. If the accidental virus is undesirable, the solution is to cut away the affected limb or simply learn to appreciate its uniqueness!

Camellia Organizations and Gardens

Help and Friends are Everywhere!

One of the best investments you will ever make in growing camellias is to join one or more of the many clubs and associations of camellia enthusiasts locally and around the world. The benefits of membership include a steady source of news and tips on growing camellias, books, literature, supplies and even plants. Plus, camellia people are some of the nicest in the world, and of the many satisfactions in life, few are more pleasurable than getting together with others to discover and exchange new ideas about a common passion. Here are some recommended organizations for camellia gardeners.

American Camellia Society

www.americancamellias.org

The ACS was founded in 1945 as the national organization of camellia enthusiasts in the United States. Its headquarters at Fort Valley, Georgia is also home to Massee Lane Gardens, which is one of the top camellia gardens in the world and encompasses nine acres of over 1,000 varieties of camellias as well as other specialty plant collections.

Membership in the ACS includes subscription to the beautiful quarterly magazine *The Camellia Journal*, as well as a copy of *American Camellia Society Yearbook*, published annually, which contains extensive articles on camellia growing. New members also receive a booklet on Camellia Culture, free admission to Massee Lane Gardens, and discounts on gifts, books and supplies from the ACS gift shop. The website is very informative with information on all aspects of growing camellias.

Memberships are available for a variety of categories and prices. Contact ACS at the website address, or The American Camellia Society, 100 Massee Lane, Fort Valley, Georgia 31030, Telephone 478-967-2358.

International Camellia Society
www.camellias-ics.org

The ICS is an international organization devoted to the genus Camellia, founded April 1962. It may be no surprise to learn that camellias are grown worldwide, including the native Asian nations, as well as Europe, Australia, New Zealand, and many other countries.

The ICS publishes a yearly journal, the *International Camellia Journal*, and it serves as the official registrar for the genus Camellia, which it maintains in the *International Camellia Register*, a multi-volume set of books.

The ICS holds an International Camellia Congress every second year at locations around the world. Regional meetings are regularly arranged by the membership representatives.

Membership is for different categories and rates vary. Contact ICS through its website which has a wealth of information.

Regional Societies

Gulf Coast Camellia Society
www.afn.org/~gccsoc
The GCCS, founded in 1962, is an association of camellia enthusiasts primarily from Alabama, Florida, Georgia, Louisiana, Mississippi, Tennessee, and Texas. It provides a forum for members to exchange region-specific information and experiences about growing camellias. The annual meeting each year in the fall includes educational programs and a plant auction where prize-winning camellias are sold.

Membership includes four issues of the quarterly magazine *Gulf Coast Camellian*, which contains articles on all aspects of camellia culture, as well as serving as an exchange of news and information among members. Contact the Gulf Coast Camellia Society through its website.

Atlantic Coast Camellia Society

http://www.atlanticcoastcamelliasociety.org/
The Atlantic Coast Camellia Society was organized in 1980 in Myrtle Beach, South Carolina. Its purpose is to extend the appreciation of Camellias and to promote the science of Camellia culture. The society has regular camellia shows and programs, and exchanges knowledge and ideas with the Camellia specialists within the membership. The ACCS is dedicated to providing information, shows and social events that you will find helpful, entertaining and enjoyable. Membership has several categories. Contact the ACCS through its website.

American Camellia Society Clubs and Societies

In addition to these organizations, the following is a list of local clubs that offer monthly meetings and programs, annual camellia shows and plant auctions, and other activities designed to help you discover more about camellias. Detailed and current information as and web sites for each of the clubs listed below is available on the American Camellia Society website. www.camellias-acs.com

Alabama
Auburn-Opelika Camellia Club
Birmingham Camellia Society
Camellia Club of Mobile
Camellia Club of South Alabama
Dothan Camellia Club
Huntsville Camellia Club

California
Atwater Garden Club & Camellia Society
Camellia Society of Kern County
Camellia Society of Modesto
Camellia Society of Sacramento
Napa Valley Camellia Society
Northern California Camellia Society
Pacific Camellia Society
Pomona Valley camellia Society
San Diego Camellia Society
San Francisco Peninsula Camellia Society
Santa Clara County Camellia Society
Southern California Camellia Society
District of Columbia, Northern Virginia, Maryland

Camellia Society of Potomac Valley

Florida
Camellia Society of Central Florida
Gainesville Camellia Society
Greater Fort Walton Camellia Society
Lakeland Camellia Society
Ocala Camellia Society
Pensacola Camellia Society
Tampa Bay Area Camellia Society
The Tallahassee Camellia Society
Georgia
Albany Camellia Club
Camellia Garden Club of Quitman
Chattahoochee Valley Camellia Society
Federated Garden Clubs of Waycross
Master Gardener's Association of SE Georgia
Middle Georgia Camellia Society
North Georgia Camellia Society
Southeastern Camellia Society
Savannah Camellia Club
Thomasville Garden Club
Valdosta Camellia Society
Louisiana
Baton Rouge Camellia Society
Camellia Club of New Orleans
Northshore Camellia Society
Ozone Camellia Club
Massachusetts
Massachusetts Camellia Society
Mississippi
Brookhaven Camellia Society

Jackson Camellia society
Mississippi Gulf Coast Camellia Society
New York
The Horticultural Alliance of the Hamptons – Camellia Group
North Carolina
Charlotte Camellia Society
Fayetteville Camellia Club
Onslow County Master Gardener Volunteers
Piedmont Triad Camellia Society
Shandhills Camellia Society
Tidewater Camellia Club
Triangle Camellia Society
Twin Rivers Camellia Society
Oregon
Oregon Camellia Society
Pennsylvania, New Jersey, Delaware, Maryland
Delaware Valley Camellia Society
South Carolina
Aiken Camellia Society
Atlantic Coast Camellia Society
Beaufort Council of Garden Clubs
Coastal Carolina Camellia Society
Grand Strand Camellia Club
Mid-Carolina Camellia Society
Texas
Coushatta Camellia Society
Virginia
Lynchburg Chapter Camellia Society
Virginia Camellia Society
International
International Camellia Society

Antiche Camelie della Lucchesia – Italy
ICS – Benelux Resions
ICS – Germany Austria
Camellias Australia, Inc.
Camellias Galacia Spain
Camellias in Japan
Kamelien in Deutchland – Germany
The New Zealand Camellia Society, Inc.
Norwegian Camellia Society
Societa' Svizzera della Camellia - Switzerland
The Rhododendron, Camellia, and Magnolia Group of the
RHS - UK

Where ever you live there is probably a camellia group near you. If there isn't, there are many ways to get in contact with club members through all the web sites listed on the ACS home page. Camellia growers are always more than happy to help with questions and you can count on them to transfer their enthusiasm about camellias. As we have said before, it can become addicting.

One group, The Pensacola Camellia Society even has a friendly service they call NCIS: Neighborhood Camellia Identification Service. They will come out and help identify camellias in your yard and give suggestions for maintaining, and growing them. That's just the kind of help you can expect from camellia growers!

Outstanding Camellia Gardens

One of the best ways to enjoy camellias is touring them in one of America's great public camellia gardens. It is surprising how many public gardens feature camellias along the

Atlantic, Pacific, and Gulf Coasts. A fine map and list can be found on the "Camellia Trail Gardens" page of the American Camellia Society official website. They are too numerous to discuss, but listed below are some "must see" camellia gardens – beginning with those nearest us of course -- which have garnered worldwide recognition for their camellia collections.

Bellingrath Gardens
12401 Bellingrath Road
Theodore, AL 36582
www.Bellingrath.org

In 1917, near Mobile, Alabama, one of Coca-Cola's early entrepreneurs, Walter Bellingrath, purchased 60 acres of riverfront near the entrance to Mobile Bay. It served only as a fishing camp for entertaining friends until he and Mrs. Bellingrath returned in 1927 from a European vacation where they had the opportunity to tour some of Europe's amazing gardens. They promptly set about to turn Bellecamp (as the fishing camp was known) into the magnificent estate and garden now known as Bellingrath Gardens. Upon its completion the garden was not open to the public. But on a Sunday afternoon in March 1932 the couple decided to open the garden for people to tour the display of camellias and azaleas. The response was more than either of them imagined, as cars seemed to line the entire 20-mile highway from Mobile to the Gardens. Seeing such great public interest, the Bellingraths decided to spend their energies making the grounds into a grand public garden of European scale. It has been open year round ever since, as visitors wander among mossy live oaks enjoying amazing garden scenes including one of America's most splendid camellia collections (Walter's favorite ornamental) some of which were purchased from homes around the region and moved to the gardens on Coca-Cola trucks!

The K. Sawada WinterGarden

Mobile Botanical Gardens
5151 Museum Drive
Mobile, AL 36689
www.mobilebotanicalgardens.org

A special attraction of the K. Sawada WinterGarden at the Mobile Botanical Gardens is its rare and significant collection of camellias developed by the region's renowned local growers. None were greater than Kosaku Sawada who famously grew a chest of seeds sent from Japan by his wife's family (as her dowry) to produce a series of cultivars that changed American camellia history. Sawada's introductions, plus hundreds more, are on display amidst a 100-acre site of gardens and longleaf pines in an unusual coastal ridge setting. It is a living monument to the region's great legacy of camellia nurserymen such as Sawada, Rubel, Kiyono, Dodd, Bellingrath, Rubel, Green, Drinkard, Bower, Jarvis, and others. The five-acre WinterGarden has many decades-old tree sized camellias including recent additions that represent the most outstanding cultivars of the last 50 years. The camellias are integrated with hollies, Japanese maples, crape myrtles and one of the world's largest collections of azalea hybrids - many of which were also developed in the Mobile area. The warm humid climate of the northern Gulf of Mexico region at Latitude 31 (roughly parallel to Interstate 10) is very favorable to outdoor growth of more tender specimens of camellia retic hybrids and new species, which are well represented here.

Burden Museum and Gardens
4560 Essen Lane
Baton Rouge, Louisiana 70809
www.discoverburden.com

One of Louisiana's hidden treasures is the Burden Museum and Gardens situated on 440 acres at Louisiana State University in the heart of Baton Rouge. Acquired by John Charles Burden in the mid 19th century and originally named Windrush Plantation, the Burden Center is home to a wide array of horticultural research projects as well as public gardens and over 3 miles of walking trails. The original camellias have now been expanded to include nearly 500 additional named varieties that once comprised the private garden of Violet Stone, whose entire collection was donated and relocated to the Burden Center in 2001. Violet and Herb Stone's garden was well known in part for its vast Higo camellia collection, as well as hundreds of collector quality varieties gathered over a lifetime. The majestic setting and outstanding collection has garnered recognition as a "Camellia Trail" garden by the American Camellia Society and an "International Garden of Excellence" by the International Camellia Society.

Massee Lane Gardens
American Camellia Society
100 Massee Lane
Ft. Valley, Georgia 31030
www.americancamellias.org

It is fitting that the headquarters of the American Camellia Society has one of the world's finest camellia collections, known as Massee Lane, filling nine acres of formal gardens between Columbus and Macon, Georgia. Massee Lane began in the 1930s as the private garden of Dave Strother. As his love for camellias grew, Strother traveled the continent gathering cuttings of the finest camellias in America, which soon filled the acreage surrounding his farmhouse. As the garden expanded, he began welcoming the public, and soon his garden became known to camellia collectors worldwide as arguably the finest private collection in North America. It is no surprise then, that after helping launch the American Camellia Society in 1945 he later donated his garden and the rest of his 150-acre farm to serve as the society's headquarters. It currently contains over 1,000 different varieties of camellias, including the best of the old and new. Massee Lane is an outdoor showcase of camellias, blooming in waves from October to March. In 1969 the large Thomas Jefferson Smith Greenhouse was built to shelter frost-tender camellia species, as well as to demonstrate the art of growing camellias under glass for the production of show-quality flowers. A regional camellia show is held at Massee Lane annually, and it has frequently hosted meetings of the American Camellia Society, including the National Show.

Magnolia Gardens
Charleston, South Carolina
www.magnoliaplantation.com

One of America's oldest and grandest gardens is found at Magnolia Plantation, which dates more than 300 years old and which played a significant role in the Revolutionary War. As the plantation has remained in the same family for over three centuries, each generation has added its own personal touch to the gardens, continually expanding its acreage and variety. The garden has over 20,000 camellias from all the main species and hybrids, including more than 150 named cultivars that were bred and named at Magnolia Gardens.

Two of the six original camellias dating from the 1800s are still in place. Within the garden are two specialty collections -- a pre-1900 camellia garden and a hybrid camellia garden. Escorted camellia walks are held daily from January to March and there are regular, well-attended educational programs on such topics as grafting, and camellia care. Research is also conducted and sponsored to locate ancient and historic camellia cultivars in the U.S. for re-propagation.

Norfolk Botanical Gardens

6700 Azalea Garden Road,
Norfolk, VA 23518
http://norfolkbotanicalgarden.org

The Norfolk Botanical Garden grew from humble beginnings as a depression-era Work Progress Administration project into a 175-acre garden now filled with thousands of plants and over 40 themed gardens. The Garden's first director, Fred Heutte, established a goal "to gather the finest collection of camellias ever presented to the American public. He may have succeeded!" The NBG collection now contains more than 1700 camellia plants including 1200 different named varieties, to which many are added each year. Approximately 750 of those plants are found in the Hofheimer Camellia Garden, established in 1992 as a joint project of the Norfolk Botanical Garden and the Virginia Camellia Society. It is named in memory of Alan and Aline Hofheimer, founding members of the Virginia Camellia Society. This garden includes 500 different types of *Camellia japonica*, 40 different types of *Camellia sasanqua* and more than 180 other species and hybrids. As a testament to the garden's quality and greatness, in 2001 the International Camellia Society named this collection one of its first ten recipients of the prestigious

"International Garden of Excellence" Award.

Descanso Gardens

1418 Descanso Drive,
La Canada Flintridge, CA 91011
www.descansogardens.org

In the foothills of the San Gabriel Mountains near Los Angeles is the former estate of newspaper publisher and entrepreneur Manchester Boddy, who in the late 1930s and 1940s carved a magnificent garden from a native live oak forest. While building his estate, then called Rancho del Descanso, he planted thousands of camellias in the shade of the oaks to provide blossoms for the cut-flower industry. When people of Japanese heritage were ordered into internment camps during World War II, Boddy purchased the entire stock of 60,000 camellias from two Japanese-owned nurseries nearby. Those and others added in later years continue to thrive, making Descanso the home of North America's largest camellia collection. It has been continually expanded to include many reticulata specimens as well as rare Camellia species, award-winning miniatures, fragrant camellias and yellow camellia hybrids. The most famous additions arrived in 1948 with the importation of 20 varieties of *Camellia reticulata* from the Kunming Institute of Botany in China. Descanso has served as host for the American Camellia Society Annual Meeting and is designated as an "International Camellia Garden of Excellence" by the International Camellia Society.

Huntington Botanical Gardens

1151 Oxford Road

159

San Marino, CA 91108

www.huntington.org

In 1903 railroad magnate Henry Huntington purchased San Marino Ranch (on the outskirts of Los Angeles), which then was a working ranch with citrus groves, nut and fruit orchards, alfalfa crops, a small herd of cows, and poultry. Today the estate, which also includes the Huntington Library and Art Museum, is home to 120 acres of spectacular gardens. The gardens contain nearly 80 different camellia species and some 1,200 named varieties. What makes this garden stand out is not only its breathtaking size and beauty, but also the number of rare and historic camellia cultivars. They include descendents of some of the earliest camellias to arrive in the US including the *Camellia japonica* 'Alba Plena' and *Camellia reticulata* 'Captain Rawes.' Perhaps the most historic plant in the collection is large *C. japonica* 'California,' believed to be the oldest camellia in Southern California. It arrived in 1888 on a tramp steamer as an unnamed seedling and was donated by the family of noted camellia collector Ralph Peer. The collection's greatness is due in large part to the work of William Hertrich, superintendent of the gardens from 1903 to 1948. New plantings of *Camellia reticulata*, first introduced to the West from China's Yunnan Province in 1948, can be seen in and around the Chinese Garden, a tribute to their native roots and to the role of the flower in Chinese culture.

Great American Camellia Gardens
Bellingrath Gardens

In 1917 Coca-Cola magnate Walter Bellingrath began sharing with friends and associates the pleasures of his "Belle Camp" fishing retreat overlooking a bend in the Isle-aux-Oies (Fowl) River, near Mobile, Alabama. He and his wife Bessie later transformed the old fish camp into what now is surely one of the most famous gardens in the world.

After a visit to Europe in 1927 the Bellingraths recruited an American architect, a French gardener, and an English landscape designer to create the beautiful Bellingrath Gardens. It opened to the public in 1932 as an enchanting scene of flowers and fountains along curving trails beneath moss-draped live oaks, magnolias, and bays. It blooms year round, best known for its dramatic display of camellias, azaleas, roses, hydrangeas, and chrysanthemums, which grow in profusion on the 800-acre estate.

The camellia was Walter Bellingrath's favorite plant. In the winters from 1935 to 1941 hundreds of stately Camellia japonicas and sasanquas, many a century old, were moved into Bellingrath Gardens. Mrs. Bellingrath and her staff, who scoured the Gulf Coast for large specimens of unusual camellias, bought them from the owners personally. The plants arrived by truck and train to fill acre after acre of the new garden.

Camellias were planted as accents at the end of vistas, some ranging 12-20 feet high with massive trunks. A Camellia Parterre displaying 100 specimen plants was staffed by employees who removed all spent blooms daily and were trained to identify each variety for visitors, as Mr. Bellingrath disliked the idea of signs marring the natural scene.

Mr. Bellingrath estimated in 1953 that more than 2,000 mature camellias of over 400 varieties graced his garden. These along with modern additions represent one of the largest collections to be found anywhere. In addition to the Camellia japonicas a large number of enormous sasanquas were planted throughout the garden.

The focal point is the Bellingrath Home, completed in 1935, which features quaint courtyards and porticoes accented by iron-lace grille work typical of the influence of old France and Spain on the Gulf Coast. For 40 years Mrs. Bellingrath collected antique furniture, priceless silver, rare porcelains and fine china, which may still be seen in the home today. A modern addition is the Boehm Gallery, which holds one of the world's largest collections of Boehm porcelains. A river cruise offers visitors a dramatic maritime excursion.

Ownership was transferred in 1950 to the Bellingrath-Morse Foundation, a non-profit trust created to perpetuate the garden for future generations. Since 1999 it has been under the able direction of Dr. William Barrick, a former President of the AHS, who grew up with camellias.

In the later years of his life, Mr. Bellingrath often expressed a desire for more and more camellia varieties. Each year, under the personal direction of Dr. Barrick, many outstanding new varieties are added, keeping the collection current with the very latest developments in the camellia world. Mr. B would be proud.

Camellia Books

Leaves about Leaves!

Camellia books are generally far more than dull instruction manuals; without exception they are fascinating snapshots of this plant for the ages, each with its own story. And the books themselves will contribute richly to your knowledge and appreciation of camellias. In fact, collecting camellia books has become an obsession in itself for many camellia enthusiasts!

The quest of many a camelliaphile is to assemble a complete set of now out-of-print American Camellia Yearbooks (1946 to present), which has led more than a few to drive hundreds of miles to a used book store, or to spend considerable sums online to obtain a complete set. There is nothing like the satisfaction of relaxing on a winter's night with an American Camellia Yearbook from the 50s or 60s. Too out of date, you say? Their advice and information is timeless. These prized yearbooks often have a pedigree of ownership and are regularly bought, shared, and traded by serious camellia enthusiasts.

A passion of many camellia growers is discovering new varieties around the globe, and camellia books often are the gateway to finding and growing them yourself. Keep your eyes open for these authors (in parentheses) when you travel to places such as England (Trehane, Anderson, Sealy), China

(Gao Jiyin), Spain, France, Italy, New Zealand (Durrant), Australia (Savige), and Japan (Tuyama). Even if you can't read the language, the photos and illustrations are worth the cost alone, often for what surely will become a future heirloom or collector's item.

Used bookstores are a great source for classic camellia books, such as those by Harold H. Hume (see listing below), a former University of Florida horticulturist who was the "George Washington" of the American camellia world. We often frequent used bookstores in cities like New Orleans, which has several that are well worth the time it takes to stop and inspect the stacks.

The American Camellia Society sells numerous books on its web site. Public garden bookstores are a good place to check. Of course, Amazon and other online retailers carry the newer titles. And online used book retailers (such as Abe Books) often carry titles no longer in print. Finally, with respect to the highly sought-after American Camellia Yearbooks, you are in luck. At least you can now find them on the ACS website for viewing by members.

Whether old books or new, and regardless your interest level, every camellia owner will find pleasure in perusing the advice and experience of experts from around the world. Below are some recommendations, both modern and classic, to keep an eye out for.

Modern Camellia Books (by date)
Camellias – The Gardener's Encyclopedia
Jennifer Trehane (Timber Press 2007)

The latest, most comprehensive book on camellias, it is beautifully written and filled with hundreds of color photos depicting various camellias and growing techniques (367 pages). Authored by Jennifer Trehane, a 2nd generation expert who is one of England's (and the world's) great authorities on camellias and a former editor of the *International Camellia Journal*.

Beyond the Camellia Belt
Dr. William L. Ackerman (Ball Publishing, 2007)
The definitive book for growing camellias in colder climates by one of the great pioneers of cold-hardy camellias, a renowned botanist with the U.S. National Arboretum. It includes lists and color photographs of suitable varieties, as well as specific advice on camellia planting and care for northern climates.

Camellias – A Practical Gardening Guide
Jim Rolfe & Yvonne Cave (Timber Press 2003)
An outstanding practical handbook (134 pages) by New Zealand camellia grower Jim Rolfe that covers all aspects of camellia growing, giving special attention to their landscape uses -- all accompanied by beautiful color images of both single blooms, and landscape scenes by professional photographer and camellia fancier Vonnie Cave.

Southern Camellias, Volumes 1, 2, 3, 4
Miles Beach (Self-published 2002-2010)
These books are a quick and handy reference for identifying camellia blooms, as they include color photographs of many named varieties, often with information about each one. They are a project of well-known camellia authority Miles Beach, who is the curator of the camellia collection at Magnolia Plantation and Gardens in Charleston.

The Illustrated Encyclopedia of Camellias
Stirling Macoboy (Timber Press, 1998)

   This book, although no longer in print, is still available from some retailers. It is an amazing and very enjoyable collection of over 1,000 photos and descriptions of the world's most popular camellias. Its coffee table format affords space for large color photos of each accompanied by an excellent description, including its history, parentage, date of origination, and flowering season.

Yunnan Camellias of China
Guomei, Lifan, Xianghon editors (Science Press 1986)

   One of the native sources of camellias is the Yunnan Province of China, home to nearly 100 species, and recent site of the International Camellia Congress. Among its specialties is the Camellia reticulata, which receives special attention in this book, filled with rich photographs. Modern methods of culture and propagation used in China are also discussed.

Camellias
Chang Hung Ta & Bruce Bartholomew (Timber Press 1984)

   This is an English translation of the 1981 monograph by H. T. Chang, published in cooperation with the American Camellia Society. Its 205 pages contain a very detailed description of nearly all species in the genus Camellia with excellent graphic illustrations, but no photographs.

The Camellia – Its History, Culture, Genetics and a Look into its Future
Dave Feathers & Milton Brown, Eds (ACS, 1978)

   No longer in print (but available used) this is a finely edited and well-illustrated compilation of articles on every aspect of camellias, each written by an expert on the subject, including (naming only a few): Ackerman, Baxter, Feathers, Hallstone, Lammerts, Nuccio, Paige, Parks, Pursel, Savige, and Trehane.

Reference Books
2014 Camellia Nomenclature
Brad King, Editor (Southern California Camellia Society)

This is the authoritative listing of all registered camellia varieties generally grown in the United States. Primarily a reference book, and updated every 2 years, it is organized by species and name, with a short description of each but no photographs. It has been adopted as the Official Nomenclature Book of the American Camellia Society.

International Camellia Registry
Neville Haydon, Registrar (International Camellia Society 2010)

This 3-volume opus is the world's most comprehensive listing of registered camellias (including the U.S.) edited by the renowned Neville Haydon of New Zealand. Besides listing all known registered varieties, it contains details and history about each (no photos), often with additional citations to other sources. It also is accessible on-line through the ICS website.

Collector Books
The Camellia Treasury – For Gardeners, Flower Arrangers and Exhibitors
Mrs. Paul Kincaid (Hearthside, New York 1964)

Camellia – Its Appreciation & Artistic Arrangement

167

CAMELLIAS BOOKS

Choka Adachi (Koyo Shoin, Tokyo 1960)

Camellias are for Everyone
Claude Chidamian (Doubleday 1959)

Camellia Culture
E. C. Tourje, ed. (MacMillan, New York 1958)

Camellias – Kinds and Culture
Harold Hume (MacMillan 1951)

Camellias and Common Sense
Claude Chidamian (Richard 1951)

Camellias Illustrated
Morrie Sharp editor (Oregon Camellia Society 1948)

Camellias in America
H. Harold Hume (McFarland 1946)

Camellias
G. G. Gerbing (Self published 1945)

Azaleas and Camellias
H. Harold Hume (MacMillan 1938)

Practical Camellia Culture
Robert J. Halliday (Baltimore 1880) (reprinted by Rubel 1945)

It's fun to start a collection and add to it. Camellia people are also generous in sharing and trading books. We are always on the lookout for old volumes and buy them to have for new members or to trade for ones we don't have. Just like collecting plants, collecting camellia books can also be addictive!

Did You Know?

- How much would you pay for a book about camellias? May we suggest *A Monograph on the Genus Camellia* by Samuel Curtis (London), published in 1819. Current price: $350,000.
- One of the most famous books about camellias is the *Iconographie du genre Camellia ou description et figures des Camellia les plus beaux et les plus rares* by Abbe Laurent Berlése (Paris) First Edition 1839. Current price: $195,050.

Sporting Camellias

An interesting phenomenon occurs when a camellia plant produces a bloom that is distinctly different in appearance from its normal color and/or form. Camellia growers call this a "sport" which results from a chromosome mutation. Camellia sports often are sufficiently unique to be propagated and distributed as an entirely new named variety.

One of the most famous sporting camellias is 'Betty Sheffield' whose chromosomes are so famously unstable that it has produced many outstanding mutations that are highly prized by collectors. Named for Mrs. Betty Sheffield of Quitman, Georgia (a "Camellia City"), the original bloom is white with occasional pink stripes. However, it has produced over two dozen named sports that would fill an entire page of the Camellia Nomenclature book.

Two famous 'Betty Sheffield' mutations are 'Betty Sheffield Supreme' (1959), a semi-double white with red-bordered petals that is among the all-time greatest. Another more recent sport is 'Elaine's Betty' (1996), which produces light pink blooms with highly ruffled petals. These or any other Betty-sports are outstanding in any garden.

Other famous sporting varieties are 'Carter's Sunburst,' 'Elegans,' 'Herme,' 'Mathotiana,' 'Tama-no-ura,' 'Tomorrow,' and 'Ville de Nantes,' to name a few. If you are fortunate to have any of those varieties, keep a close watch for unusual blooms. You may discover the next blooming sensation!

Camellia Calendar

January

- Camellia japonica blooming season is in full swing.
- Pick blooms, visit gardens, and invite friends to yours.
- Visit camellia shows to see new varieties.
- Share blooms with friends, co-workers, and the elderly.
- Excellent month for planting and transplanting camellias.
- Grafting time begins -- locate understock and scions.
- Water during dry spells and before hard freezes.
- Inspect and add mulch as necessary.
- Try waxing camellia blooms and camellia arrangements.

February

- The peak month of camellia blooming season.
- Visit camellia shows to see new varieties.
- Visit camellia gardens and invite neighbors over.
- Traditionally this is the best month for grafting.

- Water during dry spells and before hard freezes.
- As camellias finish blooming, prune for size or shape.
- An ideal month for drastic pruning and plant renovation.
- Camellias can still be easily transplanted while dormant.
- Send a soil sample for testing to determine fertilizer needs.

March

- Camellias continue blooming.
- West coast camellia shows in full swing.
- Grafting may still be done early in the month.
- As plants finish blooming, prune for shape.
- In warmer climates, begin to fertilize late in month.
- Check your irrigation system for maintenance needs.

April

- Late season blooms are winding down.
- Inspect grafts and begin hardening off as appropriate.
- Continue pruning plants for size and shape as necessary.
- Begin a fertilizing regimen if you have not already.
- Remove leaf galls from sasanquas and discard in trash.

- Spray plants for insect and scale control using summer oil.
- Water plants regularly, especially during dry periods.

May

- Camellias are growing rapidly during this month.
- Ideal month for making air layers to propagate new plants.
- Check new grafts and begin hardening as necessary.
- Water plants regularly and deeply, especially during dry spells.
- Install fresh mulch of pine straw or other suitable material.
- Pruning may still be accomplished without affecting new buds.
- Continue spraying for insects and diseases as needed.

June

- Apply a second dose of fertilizer to encourage flower buds.
- Avoid further pruning from this month forward.
- Air layers may still be made to propagate new plants.
- Continue the watering regularly and deeply.
- Install mulch if necessary to preserve moisture.
- Attend to new grafts, which should be growing and

hardening.

July

- Camellias begin budding.
- No further pruning unless absolutely necessary.
- Continue watering regimen and mulch as necessary.
- Monitor closely for insects and fungus disease for treatment.
- Begin taking cuttings for rooting throughout the month.
- Check condition of air layers for bird or insect damage.
- Plants begin entering second dormancy period.

August

- Inspect all plants for maintenance problems.
- No further pruning unless absolutely necessary.
- Continue watering regimen during hot, dry periods.
- Begin disbudding for larger blooms later in the year.
- Monitor closely for spider mites and other insect problems.
- Check condition of air layers for bird or insect damage.
- Camellias are in second dormancy, a good time to transplant.
- Continue taking cuttings for rooting from hardened new growth.

- Watch for seed pods maturing and opening late in month.

September

- Early japonicas (such as 'Arejishi') begin blooming
- Continue disbudding to promote better blooms later.
- No further pruning where flower buds are present.
- Apply light fertilizer (low nitrogen) to for bud growth.
- Continue regular watering, especially during dry periods.
- Monitor closely for spider mites and other insect problems.
- Collect mature seeds as the pods begin opening.
- Begin gibbing buds for early season blooms.

October

- Sasanqua varieties begin to bloom this month.
- Early japonica varieties are beginning to bloom.
- Continue gibbing buds for early season blooms.
- Check and treat plants for tea scale and other insects.
- Water as necessary during warm dry periods.
- Check air layers; some may be ready for potting.

November

- Camellia planting time begins.
- Early japonicas begin to bloom.

- Peak blooming season for fall sasanquas.

- Some early camellia shows (gib shows) begin.

- Check and replace mulch as necessary before winter.

- Continue gibbing blooms for holidays and camellia shows.

- Check for sources of understock for winter grafting.

- Remove air layers for potting.

- No pruning where buds are present.

December

- Ideal month for planting in the "Camellia Belt".

- Sasanquas still blooming.

- Mid-season japonicas begin blooming.

- Camellia shows are under way.

- Select camellias for Christmas gifts.

- Continue gibbing for larger blooms and camellia shows.

- Use camellias to decorate the home.

- Float camellias in bowls on dinner table.

- Try blooms in wreaths and holiday arrangements.

Holidays are great reminders of what to do when during the year. Here are a few special days to keep in mind.

Valentine's Day (February 14) ....Graft

Ides of March (March 15)..Prune

April Fools Day (April 1)........................Fertilize and spray

May Day (May 1) ....Make air layers

Summer Solstice (June 21) ....Fertilize again

Independence Day (July 4) ....Make and root cuttings

Labor Day (September 1-5)..........Gather and plant seeds

Halloween (October 31).......................... Remove air layers

Thanksgiving (late November) .... Begin planting

Christmas (December 25)............... Give camellias as gifts

New Year's Day (January 1)..........Enjoy camellia blooms

About the Authors

Forrest S. Latta is a lawyer in private practice in Mobile, Alabama. He had no idea what awaited when, at age 32, he and his wife Kathy and young family moved to an older home with large camellias, which he knew nothing about. He has served in various roles for the American Camellia Society, including as Vice-President, State Director, and Historian. He also is active in the International Camellia Society and various local camellia groups. Forrest is a certified camellia show judge who has served for many years on the state and national level.

Brenda C. Litchfield, Ph.D. - I am a professor of Instructional Design at the University of South Alabama. My husband, Jack, and I bought a house that came with over 200 mature camellias but I did not know a thing about them. I just thought - how nice it was that these big plants bloomed in the winter! I became interested in camellias after seeing a camellia show at a local mall in 2004 and the rest is history. Now the interest has turned into an obsession and Jack's favorite question is, "Where are you going to plant this one?" I regularly do waxing demonstrations which Forrest taught me years ago and grafting and air layering demonstrations to share my enthusiasm about this wonderful winter flower.

Bloom Form
Quick Reference

Single Form
Blooms of the single form are simple and generally have five to seven petals--never more than nine. Several of the beautiful Tama blooms are the single form at its best.

Semi-double Form
These flowers have two or more rows of petals. They usually have from 14 to 20 petals. The stamens are all central and conspicuous. The striking Ville De Nantes and R. L. Wheeler are good representatives of the semi-double form.

Rose Form
Petals of rose form camellias are overlapped. These can sometimes be confused with formal doubles but the clue is that with a rose form the stamens are visible when the bloom is fully open. The Purple Dawn found in so many old gardens is a rose form.

Anemone form
This form is a real standout among camellias. It is a flat flower with one or more rows of larger outer petals. The center is a convex mass of tightly packed petaloids. There are stamens intermixed with the petaloids. It's almost like two flowers in one. Elegans is a perfect example of anemone form camellias.

Peony Form
A peony form camellia is a full, beautiful bloom. It is a deep rounded flower with many rows of outer petals. The center is a convex mass of petaloids and stamens. C. M. Wilson and the old favorite Professor Sargent are good examples of peony forms.

Formal double form

The petals of a formal double spirally overlap (imbricated) and are often so perfect it's difficult to believe they are real. They often form a distinct spiral pattern from the center to the edge of the bloom. Stamens rarely show even when the bloom is fully open. Pink Perfection and Alba Plena are among the best of the formal doubles.

Common Measurements and Conversions

Basic Volume

1 teaspoon = 1⁄6 ounce

1 tablespoon = 3 teaspoons = 1/2 ounce

1/4 cup = 4 tablespoons = 2 ounces

1⁄3 cup = 5 tablespoons + 1 teaspoon d

2⁄3 cup = 10 tablespoons + 2 teaspoons

3/4 cup = 12 tablespoons = 6 ounces

1 cup = 16 tablespoons = 8 ounces

2 cups = 1 pint = 16 ounces

4 cups = 1 quart = 2 pints = 32 ounces

8 cups = 1/2 gallon = 2 quarts = 64 ounces

16 cups = 1 gallon = 4 quarts = 128 ounces

1 liter = 1.057 quarts = 34 ounces

1 peck = 8 quarts = 2 gallons

1 bushel = 4 peeks = 8 gallons

Cubic Yards and Approximate Coverage
(Mulch and other Dry Materials)

1 Cubic Yard = 27 Cubic Feet

1 Cubic Foot = 7.48 Gallons

$$\frac{\text{square feet X inches deep}}{324} = \text{cubic yards}$$

For example:

100 sq. ft. multiplied by 11/2 inches divided by 324 = .46 cubic yards

1 Cubic Yard Covers

1/2 inch deep covers 648 sq. ft.	4 inches deep covers 81 sq. ft.
1 inches deep covers 324 sq. ft.	6 inches deep covers 54 sq. ft
2 inches deep covers 162 sq. ft.	8 inches deep covers 40 sq. ft.
3 inches deep covers 108 sq. ft.	12 inches deep covers 27 sq. ft.

(Actual coverage may vary according to condition
(moisture, texture, etc.) of material. Err on the side of leftover material.)

IDEAS AND THINGS

IDEAS AND THINGS

IDEAS AND THINGS

IDEAS AND THINGS

Made in the USA
Middletown, DE
14 February 2023

24876315R00106